CULTOGRAPHIES

CULTOGRAPHIES is a new list of individual studies devoted to the analysis of cult film. The series provides a comprehensive introduction to those films which have attained the coveted status of a cult classic, focusing on their particular appeal, the ways in which they have been conceived, constructed and received, and their place in the broader popular cultural landscape. For more information, please visit www.cultographies.com

Series editors: Ernest Mathijs (University of British Columbia) and Jamie Sexton (University of Wales, Aberystwyth)

OTHER PUBLISHED TITLES IN THE CULTOGRAPHIES SERIES

BRING ME THE HEAD OF ALFREDO GARCIA

Ian Cooper

WALLFLOWER PRESS
LONDON & NEW YORK

First published in Great Britain in 2011 by

Wallflower Press,
4 Eastern Terrace Mews,
Brighton, BN2 1EP
www.wallflowerpress.co.uk

A catalogue record for this book is available from the British Library.

ISBN 978-1-906660-32-1 (pbk)

Book design by Elsa Mathern

CONTENTS

ACKNOWLEDGEMENTS

I want to thank the series editors of 'Cultographies', Ernest Mathijs and Jamie Sexton, for all of their support, advice and suggestions. It's nice to be a part of such a series.

Thanks too to Yoram Allon and all at Wallflower Press: Tom Cabot, Lucy Hurst, Elsa Mathern and Amanda O'Boyle. Particular thanks go to my good friend Jackie Downs who has helped me immeasurably over many years, particularly where this book is concerned.

I am also grateful to my wife, Julia Thaddey, for her (unpaid) proofing, her patience and her unstinting willingness to fund my chronic DVD habit.

Ian Cooper, Neuss, April 2010

This book is for my sons,
Matthew Caleb Jackson Street
and Sam Wolf Thaddey.

INTRODUCTION

THAT TITLE!

I can't remember when I first heard it. One of the great film titles, up there with *In a Lonely Place* (Nicholas Ray, 1950), *Faster, Pussycat, Kill! Kill!* (Russ Meyer, 1965) and *The Texas Chainsaw Massacre* (Tobe Hooper, 1974). Whenever I hear people talk of their loathing for Sam Peckinpah's 1974 film or their shock at its pessimism and ugliness, I always want to say 'you can't say you weren't warned'.

I knew of Peckinpah's reputation from an early age, from repeated references and admiring notices in horror magazines like *House of Hammer* and *Monster Mag*. There was the Monty Python's Flying Circus sketch, 'Sam Peckinpah's Salad Days', with its slow-motion gore, a bright young thing impaled on a tennis racket and hands chopped off by a piano lid, the stumps spouting great gouts of bright red blood. Bloody Sam. I don't know who started the game we played in the school playground but I was the one who called it Peckinpah-ing. Falling down a grassy hill, writhing in pretend pain, trying to do it all in slow-motion. I'd seen *The Wild Bunch* (1969) and *The Getaway* (1972) on TV and they'd been everything I'd expected, blood, whisky and the romance of violent death. Fast-cutting. Slow-motion. So, I expected great things when the BBC scheduled *Bring Me the Head of Alfredo Garcia* close to midnight one Friday in the late 1970s.

God. Even before the rushed ending, my sense of disappointment was crushing. It was terrible. Badly shot and hammily-acted, Warren Oates (as Bennie) all sub-Bogart mumbles and snarls. It didn't seem to make sense, I didn't know who was who and it wasn't even that violent. Worst of all, the slow-motion was perfunctory, a world away from the stylised bloody ballet of *The Wild Bunch*. Was it me? Had I missed something? It came as no surprise, therefore, that the first substantial piece I read on the film was in the 1978 book, 'The Fifty Worst Movies of All Time' by Randy Dreyfuss and Harry and Michael Medved, sharing space with *Robot Monster* (Phil Tucker, 1953), *Santa Claus Conquers the Martians* (Nicholas Webster, 1964) and *The Terror of Tiny Town* (Sam Newfield, 1938), a western with an all-midget cast. The authors seemed to pick up on all the stuff I had hated so much: the lousy plotting and the murky cinematography, the slipshod pacing and the corny dialogue (they make particular sport with the line 'you guys are definitely on my shit list'). I felt vindicated, these being the days before Michael Medved reinvented himself as the scourge of Hollywod, attacking profanity and blasphemy on talk radio and in his willfully stupid book, *Hollywood Vs. America* (1992). Indeed, Medved's enthusiastic adoption of a puritanical conservative stance suggests he may well have had motives for attacking Peckinpah other than the purely aesthetic: Medved's vision of 'America' is one not shared by the self-dubbed 'Old Iguana'. Later, when I saw *Straw Dogs* (1971) and *Cross of Iron* (1977), I put *Alfredo Garcia* down as a blot on a great director's copybook. I blamed the drink (his, not mine). Besides, it happens to a lot of great directors. Alfred Hitchcock with *Topaz* (1969); Woody Allen with *Mighty Aphrodite* (1995); Roman Polanski with *The Ninth Gate* (1999). Not to mention the ones who plummet from grace so dramatically it's frightening: Peter Bogdanovich, Bob Rafelson, Francis Coppola.

WASTE AND BEING WASTED

I've seen *Alfredo Garcia* many times in the decades since and I've realised something, realise it more with every viewing. I was wrong. The Medveds were wrong. All of the others were wrong. It is one of the great films of the 1970s. It may well be Peckinpah's masterpiece. Yes, it is a maddening film, it is ugly and messy, it is a work of 'overwhelmingly negativity' (Prince 1998: 210) and it may even be, in Mark Crispin Miller's words, 'deliberately unprepossessing' (1975: 2). But it is also unique, full of profanity and poetry, filth and beauty. It is a fever dream of a film, soaked in alcohol and with an almost hallucinatory power. Jesus, was I wrong. It is not a film for a kid. I am not talking about the violence: I was barely into my teens when I saw *The Last House on the Left* (Wes Craven, 1972), *Shivers* (David Cronenberg, 1975) and Peckinpah's own *Straw Dogs* and I loved them. That masochistic sense of making it through some sort of ordeal is a pleasurable one and one that is not affected by age: indeed, I was well into my 30s when I saw *Irréversible* (Gaspar Noé, 2002) and still felt I had achieved something by remaining in my seat until those climactic strobes started flickering. No, it is the palpable sense of decay and disillusion, the almost unbearable desperation that hangs over the film like a black cloud: that of Bennie and that of Peckinpah. It is a film stripped of the cinematic flourishes present in other films by the same director: the climactic siege in *Straw Dogs*, the bravura opening sequence of *The Getaway*, with the prison cell, the deer and the clatter of machinery, all of *The Wild Bunch*. Missing, too, is the mythic dimension so often present in

Peckinpah: the wild bunch, walking into town to fight an army or Pat Garrett shooting Billy the Kid then his own reflection in disgust. *Alfredo Garcia* is a pointedly squalid film, where drink is an anaesthetic, violence is not redemptive and formal considerations like pacing, editing and lighting are secondary to this pervasive sense of waste. That, in the end, is what it comes down to: waste. It is important to avoid the suggestion that because a film is (technically) bad, it's good, a lack of proficiency being some sort of guarantee of 'authenticity' (although there are cult film fans who would argue such a thing, citing the likes of Andy Milligan, the Kuchar brothers or Herschell Gordon Lewis). But film is a conservative medium, being (until recently, at least) prohibitively expensive and with production and distribution traditionally being the preserve of big corporations. Given this, unregulated free expression is much rarer than it is in other artistic disciplines and consequently, there are few instances where a talented filmmaker so blatantly chronicles his damaged psyche, his rage, even his own decline, artistic and otherwise. Maybe Pier Paolo Pasolini's *Salo* (1975), a decadent film from a man at the end of his string, reeking of death and sex. Or *Bad Lieutenant* (Abel Ferrara, 1992), a druggy raw wound of a film, with Harvey Keitel's performance equal parts astonishing and embarrassing: critic Gavin Smith suggests that the latter film 'is to Ferrara what another masterpiece, *Bring Me the Head of Alfredo Garcia* was to Sam Peckinpah, in precisely the same hardboiled tradition of personal/artistic/spiritual statement' (1993: 21). Perhaps the best comparison is with *Frenzy* (1972), Hitchcock's last masterpiece, a slice of self-autopsy, widely misunderstood at the time of its initial release (this comparison is explored further in chapter 4).

CULT CINEMA AND OPPOSITION

Certain terms frequently recur in discussions of cult cinema, terms such as oppositional, transgressive and plain bad with a film's cultish credentials often being measured by its distance from the mainstream. For Jeffrey Sconce, cult audiences promote:

their tastes and textual proclivities in opposition to a loosely defined group of cultural and economic elites, those purveyors of the status quo who not only rule the world, but who are also responsible for making the contemporary cinema … so completely boring. (2003: 103)

In their introduction to *The Cult Film Reader*, Ernest Mathijs and Xavier Mendik suggest that:

Beyond the basic poles of good and bad, a lot of the competence of a cult film lies in its ability to transgress the barriers of good and bad; to obliterate them. A common way of achieving this is through the challenging of one or more 'conventions' of filmmaking, which may include stylistic, moral or political qualities … defying more consensual logistics of narrative construction. (2003a: 2)

This oppositional, transgressive quality can be a matter of content, as in the violent horror films of Ruggero Deodato and Lucio Fulci or the stylised hardcore porn of Radley Metzger and the Mitchell brothers, the acid movies of the 1960s or the 'New Queer Cinema' of the 1990s. Sometimes, it may be a question of form, as in the undergound movies of Kenneth Anger or the homemade nightmares of *Eraserhead* (David Lynch, 1977) and *Nekromantik* (Jörg Buttgereit, 1987).

Indeed, John Waters' *Pink Flamingos* (1972), a zero-budget mix of coprophilia, blow-jobs and chicken-killing ticks all the cult boxes. A smaller sub-category are those films where traditional notions of quality are undermined and incompetence is a virtue. Examples of this include the work of Ed Wood, Al Adamson or the more *outré* work of Jess Franco (such as *Barbed Wire Dolls* (1975), where the slow-motion scenes are achieved by having actors move very slowly). But *Alfredo Garcia* stands alone, representing as it does a spectacular fall from grace as a director seen as a possible heir to John Ford, admired by Akira Kurosawa and Federico Fellini, so spectacularly screws up. There have always been films from acclaimed directors that have misfired, from Otto Preminger's *Skidoo* (1968), with a tripping Burgess Meredith and Groucho Marx as God to Robert Altman's *Popeye* (1980). But these films are often regarded as aberrations whereas Peckinpah's film led critics to question his judgement, his talent and even his sanity.

Any serious consideration of cult cinema takes in a bewildering variety of material, encompassing films that are weird, strange, innovative and nasty, quirky, passionate and personal, sometimes defiantly so while others seem to amount to demented accidents, and all with a devoted fanbase. These films offer up a shadow history of film: F. W. Murnau and Tod Browning, James Whale and Edgar Ulmer, Robert Hamer and Henri-Georges Clouzot, Phil Karlson and Sam Fuller, Roger Corman and Mario Bava, Monte Hellman and Peter Watkins, Lucio Fulci and Nicolas Roeg, Jerzy Skolimovski and Takashi Miike and Gaspar Noé. Don't forget the misfires and the oddities from acclaimed filmmakers: Hitchcock's *The Wrong Man* (1956), John Huston's *Reflections in a Golden Eye* (1967), Billy Wilder's *The Private Life of Sherlock Holmes* (1970), Michael Cimino's *Heaven's Gate* (1980). And the one-offs, the freakish and the plain mad: *A Page of Madness* (Kinugasa Teinosuke,

1926), *White Zombie* (Victor Halperin, 1933), *Strange Cargo* (Frank Borzage, 1940), *Nightmare Alley* (Edmund Goulding, 1947), *Carnival of Souls* (Herk Harvey, 1962), *La Maman et la Putain* (Jean Eustache, 1974), *The Stunt Man* (Richard Rush, 1980), *Paganini* (Klaus Kinski, 1989), *The Young Poisoner's Handbook* (Benjamin Ross, 1995). All of the above films and filmmakers offer something unique, whether strange or sad, striking or stupid. Unlike so many other films, in or out of the mainstream, there is always room for what David Lynch, interviewed for the 1993 documentary *Made in the USA*, described as 'an abstraction or a dream'. I don't know if *The Honeymoon Killers* (Leonard Kastle, 1969) was supposed to be so strange, both campy and horrific, amateurish and assured. Was future soft-porn auteur Zalman King winging it in *Blue Sunshine* (Jeff Lieberman, 1976) or was his bizarre performance actually directed? Did Ted Post want to create something as unique as *The Baby* (1972), a too-sick-to-be-funny, too-funny-to-be-scary freak-out with big hair, wacky outfits and an unforgettable ending? Or did something just happen along the way, to warp a nasty little melodrama into something else? How did anyone come up with something as freakish as *Café Flesh* (1982), a hardcore-porn sci-fi film written by Jerry Stahl (celebrity junkie and creator of television's cat-eating alien *Alf* (1986–89)) and directed by Rinse Dream? And how the hell can anyone sit through the inept poetry of Ed Wood's films and fail to see them as a striking example of warped autobiography, their director kin to Sam Fuller and David Lynch?

Jeffrey Sconce's notion of paracinema is a useful one in this context, a category which enthusiastically embraces such cinematic detritus as:

badfilm, splatter-punk, 'mondo' films, sword and sandal epics, Elvis flicks, government hygiene films, Japanese monster movies, beach-party musicals, and just about every other historical manifestation of exploitation cinema from juvenile delinquency documentaries to soft-core pornography. (2003: 101)

For Sconce (who is nothing if not provocative) the 'histrionic, anachronistic and excessive' (2003: 118) paracinema offers pleasures that 'academy icons such as Sirk and Godard' (ibid.) can not. Indeed, he suggests that such oddball fare as *Zontar the Thing from Venus* (Larry Buchanan, 1966) and *The Corpse Grinders* (Ted V. Mikels, 1972) may come closer to embodying Bertolt Brecht's conception of an anti-illusionist aesthetic than Douglas Sirk's *Written on the Wind* (1955) or Jean-Luc Godard's *Tout va bien* (1972). While not wishing to place Peckinpah alongside Larry Buchanan, the tension between 'the academy' and the cult canon that is so important to paracinema is worth applying to *Alfredo Garcia*. For Sconce:

> While the academy prizes conscious transgression of conventions by a filmmaker looking to critique the medium aesthetically and/or politically, paracinematic viewers value a stylistic and thematic deviance born, more often than not, from the systematic failure of a film aspiring to obey dominant codes of cinematic representation. (2003: 112)

Bring Me the Head of Alfredo Garcia demonstrates either or both of these seemingly-contradictory positions simultaneously.

Cult films can scar, leave a mark, cause images to rise out of the subconscious years later like Romero zombies, images that can thrill, amuse, revolt. Some, like Peckinpah's coruscating blend of romance and nihilistic rage, manage to do all three things at the same time. *Bring Me the Head of Alfredo Garcia* is a film full of vivid moments, many of them etched on my mind like an acid flashback: a topless, heavily-pregnant woman having a bone snapped. A couple sitting under a tree by the side of the road, drinking. A gleaming machete. A slo-mo spade swinging out of the dark. A shot man, doing a spastic roll and ending up back on his feet. A severed head, crawling with flies, soaked in tequila, steaming under a hot shower. A freeze-framed gun barrel, this big black circle signifying nothing. You might not like Peckinpah's film, but I don't think you'll forget it.

One more thing. When I was a teenager, I had a friend who bore serious mental scars from years of heavy amphetamine abuse. On one occasion, we watched an hour of the rock mockumentary *The Rutles: All You Need is Cash* (Eric Idle/Gary Weis, 1978) together before he snorted dismissively that the eponymous band were 'just ripping off the Beatles'. Once, in the middle of a stoned late-night conversation, he said, 'I saw this film the other night. Bring Me Some Fucker's Head.' I nodded. 'I know that film. Bring Me the Head of Alfredo Garcia. Sam Peckinpah.' He thought about it for a while. 'No. This was definitely Bring Me Some Fucker's Head.'

1

'YOU GUYS ARE DEFINITELY ON MY SHIT LIST': PRODUCTION, PROMOTION, INITIAL RECEPTION

PECKINPAH AND 1970s CINEMA

Peckinpah, along with directors such as Arthur Penn, Stanley Kubrick and Robert Altman, can be regarded as a transitional figure in American cinema, bridging the gap between 1950s auteurs like Robert Aldrich, Nicholas Ray and Elia Kazan and the later 'Movie Brats' of the 1970s. This was the first generation of directors to work in television. They were also the first wave of American directors to be demonstrably influenced by foreign (that is, non-Hollywood) cinema:[1] Altman openly lifted from Ingmar Bergman for *Images* (1972), and *Bonnie and Clyde* (1967) passed from Jean-Luc Godard to François Truffaut before ending up with Arthur Penn.

The critical reappraisal of a number of studio system-era directors that had begun in France and spread to the US was also a contributing factor to the vibrant film culture of the 1950s and 1960s, with the auteur theory positing that it was possible to make personal films in the factory-like context of Hollywood. In a piece on *Bonnie and Clyde*, Philip French quotes the film's screenwriters, Robert Benton and David Newman, who accurately sum up this heady period:

> We were riding the crest of a new wave that had swept in on our minds, and the talk was Truffaut, Godard, DeBroca, Bergman, Kurosawa, Antonioni, Fellini and all the other names that fell like a litany in 1964, along with the sudden and staggering heights of rediscovery around the pantheon people – Hitchcock, Hawks, Ford, Welles and the rest. (2007)

Accordingly, Peckinpah's work is influenced by the twin traditions of Hollywood genre filmmaking and auteur cinema from Europe and beyond. Among the directors he expressed admiration for are Huston, Wilder, John Ford and George Stevens as well as Bergman, Kurosawa and Alain Resnais (see Seydor 1980: 266). Peckinpah and his contemporaries began by making what were more or less conventional genre films and moved on to a more experimental, expressive style throughout the 1960s and into the 1970s. The evolution in Peckinpah's filmmaking, from *Ride the High Country* (1962) to *Alfredo Garcia* is mirrored in the work of Penn, Kubrick and Altman: compare *The Delinquents* (Altman, 1957) to *Nashville* (1975), *The Killing* (Kubrick, 1956) to *A Clockwork Orange* (1971) or *The Miracle Worker* (Penn, 1962) to *Night Moves* (1975).

For some years now, the pre-*Star Wars* (George Lucas, 1977) director-friendly 1970s have been mythologised as a time of unprecedented freedoms (see Corrigan 1991, Kolker 2000, or, for a more gossipy account, Biskind 1998). The fall-off in cinema audiences from the mid-1960s onwards and the emergence of the counterculture led to a period of uncertainty for the film industry, with a new generation of directors and producers taking advantage of this temporary crisis. Producers such as Robert Evans and Bert Schneider and directors including Coppola, Bogdanovich, Martin Scorsese, William Friedkin, Bob Fosse and Hal Ashby managed to build careers making recognisably personal films. The pre-VCR tradition of the 'midnight movie' saw oddball talents such as George Romero, Alejandro Jodorowsky and John Waters find an audience. In the wake of *Night of the Living Dead* (Romero, 1968), the American horror film moved into a new golden age, wherein vampires and monsters were replaced by cannibal families in *The Texas Chainsaw Massacre* and *The Hills Have Eyes* (Wes Craven, 1977). The decade also saw a number of veterans coming up with some weird, off-beat projects that took full advantage of both the industrial uncertainty of the times and the collapse of the Production Code. Consider the heated Southern Gothic of *The Beguiled* (from Peckinpah mentor, Don Siegel, 1971). Or the drunks and washed-up boxers of *Fat City* (John Huston, 1972). Arthur Penn's wacky westerns, *Little Big Man* (1970) with a centenarian Dustin Hoffman and *The Missouri Breaks* (1976) with a cross-dressing, psychotic Marlon Brando. Or the bleak and grimy *Hustle* (Robert Aldrich, 1975) which teamed Burt Reynolds with Catherine Deneuve. Even a hack like Arthur Hiller came up with *The Hospital* (1971), an impressive adaptation of a characteristically sour Paddy Chayevsky script. But even in the freewheeling 1970s, this (last?) Golden Age of American movies, this period of 'pessimism and permissiveness' (Mathijs 2008: 30), Peckinpah had difficulty making films free of studio interference.

From his little-seen debut film *The Deadly Companions* (1961) on, his fortunes had been distinctly mixed. His second film, *Ride the High Country*, received some excellent reviews but the would-be epic *Major Dundee* (1964) was butchered by the studio. After being fired from the Steve McQueen vehicle *The Cincinatti Kid* that same year (after only four days of shooting) he was blacklisted for years before a triumphant comeback with *The Wild Bunch*. By 1974, his stock had fallen considerably, despite the commercial success of *The Getaway*. The uncharacteristically gentle *The Ballad of Cable Hogue* (1970) had been a flop and *Straw Dogs*, while successful, had proved a turn-off to many and divided critics: Pauline Kael infamously dubbed it 'the first American film that is a fascist work of art' (quoted in Fine 2005: 210). Added to this was his growing (some would say hard-earned) reputation as an angry drunk who was loath to compromise. His last picture prior to *Alfredo Garcia*, *Pat Garrett and Billy the Kid* (1973), made for MGM, had been taken away from him, savagely re-cut and released to poor box office and terrible reviews (the *New Republic* considered that 'this stale saga is dull, slow and sillily portentous', while for *Newsweek*, it was 'a mis-shapen mess' (quoted in Fine 2005: 260)). The reasons for this will be discussed in more depth later but James Aubrey, the Head of Production at MGM, had become another hate figure for Peckinpah, no stranger to meddling studios and producers. Aubrey was the most recent in a long line of sleazy, greedy suits who screwed him and mangled his movie ('The saying is they can kill you but not eat you. That's nonsense. I've had them eating on me while I was still walking around' (Peckinpah quoted in Butler 1979: 8)). This depressing experience had exacerbated the drinking that had been a problem for most of his adult life. It also encouraged the self-pitying view Peckinpah had of himself, not without foundation, as a great artist beset by moneymen and philistines. *Alfredo Garcia* was his attempt to make a film without compromises, making no concessions, either to United Artists (UA) or the audience. The budget of $1.5 million was low and it shows onscreen: for the novelist Rick Moody, the film is 'more like the B-films of Roger Corman than John Ford' (2009).

GENESIS

The genesis of the film came from Frank Kowalski, an old friend of the director. During the shooting of *The Ballad of Cable Hogue*, Kowalski brought Peckinpah the bare bones of a story about a bartender who is sent by a Mafia don to cut the head off a corpse. Kowalski was also interested in the story of Caryl Chessman. Known as 'The Red Light Bandit', Chessman was a charismatic robber and rapist who wrote a number of best-selling books during a ten-year stretch on Death Row before his execution in 1960.

The script was worked on over the next three years with Kowalski dropping out and Gordon Dawson taking his place. Interviewed for Tom Thurman's feature documentary *Sam Peckinpah's West* (2004), Dawson claimed he ended up writing the final version of the script in ten days and was paid $10,000. Even a cursory glance at the credits of Kowalski and Dawson tells us a lot about the oddball pedigree of the film. Kowalski had an uncredited bit part in the James Cagney film *Angels with Dirty Faces* (Michael Curtiz, 1938) and had worked in various capacities on an eclectic mix of projects: script supervising for *The Outer Limits* television show (1963–65) and providing continuity on the cult film *Sex Kittens Go To College* (Albert Zugsmith, 1960) starring Mamie Van Doren and Conway Twitty 'as himself'. His only previous screenwriting credit was for the western *A Man Called Sledge* (1970), which he co-wrote with the director/star, Vic Morrow. But his 'dialogue supervisor' credit on *The Ballad of Cable Hogue* may be misleading. According to the star of the film, Jason Robards, Kowalski was responsible for 'anything [in the script] that was funny or had real humour. Frank was invaluable to Sam. He had a mind' (in Fine 2005: 164).

Dawson had been a part of Peckinpah's circle since *Major Dundee*. He had worked on five of the director's films, moving from costume and wardrobe to second unit director on *The Getaway* to screenwriter and associate director. During the *Alfredo Garcia* shoot, he walked off the set, disgusted by Peckinpah's behaviour and vowing never to work with the director again:

> He really lost it on *Alfredo* ... I had him up there on the pedestal. My fault for putting him up there, you know, that's a tough place to be but he sure fell off on that picture and I couldn't put Humpty Dumpty back together again in my mind. (In Weddle 1994: 494)

Dawson has worked mainly in television since then, writing for popular shows like *The Rockford Files* (1974–80), *Diagnosis Murder* (1993–2001) and *Baywatch Nights* (1995–97).

Much has been made of Peckinpah's struggles with producers and moneymen of all stripes (take Marshall Fine's statement that, after *Major Dundee*, the director 'was even more convinced that producers were not a necessary evil – they were just plain evil' (2005: 101)). But his relationship with Martin Baum, the producer of *Alfredo Garcia*, was an unusually long-lasting and productive one. Baum had been the President of ABC Pictures and helped bring a number of impressive projects to the screen, including *The Grissom Gang* (Robert Aldrich, 1971), *Cabaret* (Bob Fosse, 1972) and *Straw Dogs*, before he went on to form his own production company, Optimus, with financing from United Artists. Although his relationship with Peckinpah soured during the shoot of the 1975 film *The Killer Elite* (largely due to the latter's new-found enthusiasm for cocaine), when Baum joined Creative Artists Agency, he became the director's agent.

CASTING: OATES ET LES AUTRES

The casting was untypical for a Peckinpah film as it contained few members of his regular stock company of actors (such as Strother Martin, L. Q. Jones, E. G. Marshall), many of whom had been with him since his television work in the 1950s. It does, however, bring to mind the comment made about the cast of *The Man Who Fell to Earth* (Nicolas Roeg, 1975): 'That's a dinner party, not a cast' (thevoid99: 2007). For the lead role, Peckinpah had first approached his friend and frequent collaborator James Coburn, but Coburn hated the idea ('I said, why would you want to do this?' (in Fine 2005: 268)). Peter Falk, TV cop *Columbo* (1968–97) and a member of the John Cassavetes stock company, was interested but too busy. It is no surprise that Peckinpah ended up casting Warren Oates as Bennie. The Kentucky-born actor was a Peckinpah veteran, appearing in *Ride the High Country*, *Major Dundee* and *The Wild Bunch*, as well as the television show, *The Rifleman* (1958–63). Oates was a major talent and a significant figure in 1970s Hollywood. He featured in three impressive directorial debuts, *The Hired Hand* (Peter Fonda, 1971) *Badlands* (Terrence Malick, 1973) and *Dillinger* (John Milius, 1973) as well as a number of films for cult director (and Peckinpah friend/collaborator) Monte Hellman. He also appeared in films by Friedkin, Steven Spielberg, Norman Jewison and Phil Kaufman. Like Peckinpah, he had served as a Marine and was a heavy drinker. He was also a versatile actor who possessed a kind of greasy, anti-glamour: he expressed surprise at his frequent appearances in westerns, 'because my image of the western man is John Wayne and I'm just a little shit' (quoted in Neumaier 2004). The critic David Thomson is an Oates fan, writing about him in 1981, the year the actor died:

Oates seems at first sight grubby, balding, and unshaven. You can smell whiskey and sweat on him, along with that mixture of bad beds and fallen women. He's toothy, he's small, he's 53 this year, and he has a face like prison bread, with eyes that have known too much solitary confinement. (2002b: 642)

Thomson's fellow critic, Michael Sragow, was another admirer, suggesting that the actor could:

Glower, furrow his brow and pull in his lip as skilfully as Fred Astaire could dance and Cary Grant could grin … Even in an age of easy riders and easy pieces, Oates' confusion had special resonance. His scowl, which could suggest anything from bereavement to amusement, most often signalled a mixture of anger, befuddlement and defeat in the midst of a modern world that was passing beyond any individual's power of understanding. (2000a)

In the documentary feature *Warren Oates: Across the Border* (Tom Thurman, 1993), actor Ned Beatty, is almost euphemistic, describing Oates as playing 'negative' guys, while Robert Culp calls him 'a glorious failure that demands our love and respect'. Director Richard Linklater was unequivocal in his appreciation when he wrote 'there was once a god who walked the earth named Warren Oates' (2008). *Alfredo Garcia* was one of only three leading roles Oates played, out of the fifty or so films he made. Oates said of Peckinpah, 'I don't think he's a horrible maniac; it's just that he injures your innocence and you get pissed off about it' (quoted in Thomson 2002b: 642). He openly acknowledged the director's influence on his performance as Bennie: 'I tried to say it all: what I knew about Sam and his love for Mexico. I really tried to do Sam Peckinpah: as much as I know about him, his mannerisms and everything he did' (in Bomar and Warren 1981). This stretched to wearing Peckinpah's sunglasses. Placing Oates in the role of surrogate-Sam makes it explicit that the self-pity and disgust that runs through the film is that of the director and what we see in the film is one drunken loser in sunglasses, chasing hopeless dreams of success south of the border, making a film about another drunken loser in (the same pair of) sunglasses.

Peckinpah reportedly auditioned a number of actors for the role of Elita before casting Isela Vega. She had been a model and singer before becoming an actor, appearing in many Mexican movies, including the evocatively-titled *Cuernos debajo de la cama/Cuckolded Under the Bed* (Ismael Rodriguez, 1969), *Las luchardoras contra el robot asesino/Wrestling Women versus the Murderous Robot* (René Cardona, 1969) and *El Sabor de la Vengenza/Taste of the Savage/* (Alberto Mariscal, 1971). She pulls off the difficult role of Elita, a sexy, frequently topless singer/whore who both loves and betrays Bennie. She also wrote 'Bennie's Song', which she performs on their fateful car journey. Two years after *Alfredo Garcia*, she was reunited with Oates in *Drum* (Steve Carver, 1976), the sequel to *Mandingo* (Richard Fleischer, 1975). She went on to write and direct the occult thriller, *Los Amantes del senor de la noche/Lovers of the Lord of the Night* (1986), starring alongside Emilio 'El Indio' Fernandez.

Fernandez was cast as the brutal patriarch, El Jefe. He was a frequent Peckinpah collaborator, notably in the role of Mapache in *The Wild Bunch*. 'El Indio' is a towering figure in Mexican cinema, a larger-than-life character onscreen and off. In the 1920s, he escaped from prison while serving a twenty-year stretch for his role in the Heurista rebellion. As an actor, he worked for John Huston (*Night of the*

Robert Webber and Gig Young as Sappensly and Quill

Iguana (1964)) and Polanski (*Pirates* (1986)) and co-starred with John Wayne (*Chisum* (Andrew McLaglen, 1970)) and Marlon Brando (*The Appaloosa* (Sydney J. Furie, 1966)). He was also a noted screenwriter and the director of 43 films, including *Maria Candelaria* (1944), which won the Grand Prize at Cannes in 1946. Fernandez was the subject of a number of rumours, such as the claim that he was the model for the Oscar statuette (see Ostrand 2006) and that he shot a critic in the balls. Two years after *Alfredo Garcia*, he was convicted of manslaughter after killing a farm labourer. Given this reputa-tion, it is no surprise that people found Fernandez frightening. Peckinpah's assistant and on/off girlfriend Katy Haber called him 'a poet, a writer, a director, a womaniser, a drinker and a murderer' (in Fine 2005: 270) and Gordon Dawson wasn't im-pressed: 'He'd pistol whip people just to watch them bleed. Sam was not an evil man like this guy was' (in ibid.). Robert Webber and Gig Young play the gay bounty-hunters who re-cruit and then double-cross Bennie. Although un-named in the film, in the script they sport the splendidly-Dickensian names Sappensly and Quill. Webber is probably best-known as Juror Number 12 in *Twelve Angry Men* (Sidney Lumet, 1957).

Like Peckinpah and Oates, he had served in the Marines. A veteran character actor, he had appeared in *Harper* (Jack Smight, 1966), *The Dirty Dozen* (Robert Aldrich, 1967) and a lot of television shows including *The Outer Limits*, *Mission: Impossible* (1966–73) and *Kojak* (1973–78). He had worked with Peckinpah years earlier, in an episode of *The Rifleman*.

Born Byron Barr, Young was best known for supporting roles in lightweight fare, such as *Young at Heart* (Gordon Douglas, 1954) and *That Touch of Mink* (Delbert Mann, 1962). He excelled, however, in the untypical role of the desiccated MC in *They Shoot Horses, Don't They?* (Sydney Pollack, 1969) and won a Supporting Actor Academy Award for the role. But by the 1970s, he was beset by myriad personal problems, including a debilitating drink problem: he was fired from his role as the Waco Kid in *Blazing Saddles* (Mel Brooks, 1974) due to a bad case of the shakes. Peckinpah cast Young when his original choice for the role, the satirical comedian Mort Sahl, dropped out. Four years after the film, in September 1978, a *Washington Post* profile called him 'blithe as ever, a survivor [who] is frustrating the Curse of the Oscar' (quoted in Anon. 1994). Less than a month later, Young was dead, shooting himself after killing his fifth wife of three weeks, 21-year-old actor Kim Schmidt. To the end, the actor was aware of the debt of gratitude he owed to *Alfredo Garcia*'s Martin Baum, who, as his agent, had lobbied tirelessly on his behalf. He bequeathed his Academy Award to Baum, who would go on to describe Young as seeming 'like a man who had everything going for him. How little we know' (quoted in Anon. 2004). It may be hindsight, but his dead-eyed performance in Peckinpah's film is chilling, his eerie smile and hangdog face lined by alcohol and disappointment.

Helmut Dantine was cast as Max, a cold-blooded El Jefe crony. Dantine was an Austrian who came to America in the late 1930s after his anti-Nazi activities led to him spending three months in a concentration camp. He had an uncredited part in *Casablanca* (Michael Curtiz, 1942) and, like many European refugees of the time, he often played Nazis (in *Mrs Miniver* (William Wyler, 1942) and *Edge of Darkness* (Lewis Milestone, 1943)). In addition to his acting duties, he was an executive producer on *Alfredo Garcia* and *The Killer Elite* and, in what was no doubt a bit of wish fulfilment on Peckinpah's part, he is shot dead in both. Kris Kristofferson plays the Charles Mansonish biker who abducts Elita before being killed by Bennie. He had been a Rhodes scholar and a helicopter pilot in the US army before becoming a songwriter, working with artists including Johnny Cash and Jerry Lee Lewis. He went on to have a successful career as a singer/songwriter and is best known for the songs 'Me and Bobby McGee' and 'Help Me Make It Through The Night' (both 1969). After popping up in Dennis Hopper's chaotic *The Last Movie* (1971), he starred as a singing drug-dealer in *Cisco Pike* (Bill L. Norton, 1972). *Alfredo Garcia* was his second Peckinpah film, following his turn as Billy the Kid in *Pat Garrett and Billy the Kid*. He went on to appear in the smash hit 1970s version of *A Star is Born* (Frank Pierson, 1976) before taking the lead in the shambolic *Convoy* (1978). Since then, in addition to his recording career, Kristofferson has featured in a number of interesting projects (*Heaven's Gate*, *Limbo* (John Sayles, 1999), *The Jacket* (John Maybury, 2005)) as well as some shoddy commercial fare (alongside fellow Peckinpah veteran James Coburn in *Payback* (Brian Helgeland, 1999) and *Planet of the Apes* (Tim Burton, 2001)). In 1975, he recorded the song 'Rocket to Stardom' with Warren Oates providing backing vocals. Donnie Fritts played keyboards in Kristofferson's band and he was cast as the other biker. He crops up in *Pat Garrett and Billy the Kid* and *Convoy*, as well as *Cockfighter* (Monte Hellman, 1974) opposite Oates. Other Peckinpah cronies turn up, some in wordless cameos. Katy Haber, the actors Don Levy and Richard Bright and the director's eldest daughter Sharon all make appearances.

CREW: PECK AND THE PACK

The cinematographer was the Mexican Alex Phillips Jr. His Russian father was 'a legend of Mexican cinema' (Davison 2007), a prolific cinematographer with 202 film credits, including Luis Buñuel's *Robinson Crusoe* (1954). Phillips Jr was no slouch, either, working on more than one hundred films including Ralph Nelson's weird western *The Wrath of God* (1972), George C. Scott's overheated Oedipal drama *The Savage is Loose* (1974) and the box-office smash *Romancing the Stone* (Robert Zemeckis, 1984). His work on *Alfredo Garcia* is certainly distinctive, from the effectively scuzzy (the scenes in Bennie's room at the start of the film) to the idyllic (the sunny drive through the countryside) to the awful, particularly the mismatched lighting after Bennie kills the bikers. In fact, much of the disorientation of the film's first half comes from the way the lighting appears to change from shot to shot, offering the most dislocated cinematography in a studio film since Russ Meyer's demented *Beyond the Valley of the Dolls* (1970). While Phil Davison considers that 'the lens perfectly captures Peckinpah's vision of an alcohol-induced feverish dream' (2007), Richard T. Jameson and Kathleen Murphy's (euphemistic?) description of the cinematography as 'eerily poor' (1981: 45) is nearer the mark.

The music was by the frequent Peckinpah collaborator Jerry Fielding, who worked with the director on six projects, starting with the television play *Noon Wine* (1966). Particularly noteworthy are his brooding, atmospheric scores for *The Wild Bunch* and *Straw Dogs*. After an investigation by the House Committee on Un-American Activities, Fielding had been blacklisted in Hollywood for much of the 1950s but made a high-profile comeback with his work on *Advise and Consent* (Otto Preminger, 1962). He would go on to score pictures for Karel Reisz (*The Gambler* (1974)), Donald Cammell (the cult sci-fi film *Demon Seed* (1977)) and Don Siegel (*Escape from Alcatraz* (1979)), as well as regular collaborations with Michael Winner and Clint Eastwood. Unsurprisingly, his relationship with Peckinpah did not always go smoothly: after Steve McQueen junked Fielding's score for *The Getaway*, the composer turned down the chance to work with Bob Dylan on *Pat Garrett and Billy the Kid*. His music for *Alfredo Garcia* is magnificent, albeit strikingly odd: in places it is so over-emphatic, it almost comes across as parodic, ranging from lush string arrangements and horror movie discord via some faux-mariachi noodling. But this eclectic approach actually works in a film so stylistically excessive, with the music matching the artless framing and cluttered *mise-en-scène* perfectly. Particularly effective is the use of muzak in upmarket hotel scenes, tacky music for El Jefe's tacky hoods. When Bennie opens fire, killing everyone in the room, the tinny, upbeat sounds serve as an ironic counterpoint, an idea later used by George Romero in his *Dawn of the Dead* (1978). Fielding died young (aged 58) of heart failure, as would Peckinpah (at 59) and Oates (53).

THE SHOOT, RELEASE AND INITIAL RECEPTION

Peckinpah shot the film in Mexico, in Mexico City and Cuernavaca. He had a long, ambivalent relationship to the country, and in his work it often seems to represent both a heaven and a hell, a site of innocence and a primitive place of violent death – a surrogate Vietnam, perhaps. He said of *Alfredo Garcia*, it 'couldn't have been made anywhere else' (in Madsen 1974: 91) The shoot was a difficult one, although this wasn't unusual for a Peckinpah film: on *Major Dundee* he had been attacked by a sabre-wielding Charlton Heston, fired 35 members of the crew on *The Ballad of Cable Hogue*, caught pneumonia after a Lands End drinking binge on *Straw Dogs*, pissed his name on the dailies of *Pat Garrett and Billy the Kid* and was often too out of it to work at all on *Convoy*. These kind of stunts led Garrett Chaffin-Quiray to suggest (slightly euphemistically) that Peckinpah used 'a kind of out-of-control creative experience whereby directors harangue, terrorise and otherwise influence actors to give electric performances' (2007: 282). During his intermittent periods off the booze, Peckinpah was smoking a lot of dope and spent much of his time in his trailer, hooked up to an IV drip.

When UA executives saw the film, they were horrified. Fearing it would earn a commercially disastrous X rating, they considered not releasing it at all. The previews were terrible. One ended with only ten viewers left in the cinema. The responses on the preview cards included 'the most terrible movie I've ever seen' (quoted in Prince 1998: 149), 'to put that inhuman mess on film is a crime' (quoted in ibid.), 'this picture should be burned' (quoted in Prince 1998: 227) and 'it doesn't relate to my life or anyone else's' (quoted in ibid.). The reviews were even worse. For the *Wall Street Journal*:

> So grotesque in its basic conception, so sadistic in its imagery, so irrational in its plotting, so obscene in its effect, and so incompetent in its cinematic realisation that the only kind of analysis it really invites is psychoanalysis. (Quoted in Prince 1998: 195)

New York magazine called it 'a catatastrophe' (quoted in Ebert 2001); *Variety* wrote that it was 'turgid melodrama at its worst' (quoted in ibid.). Vincent Canby suggested that all of Peckinpah's previous films should be reappraised in the light of this 'disaster' (1974). For the *New York Times*, it was 'a film portrait of pessimism' with Oates 'blustery … frantic', Vega 'awkward', Young, Kristofferson and Dantine 'wasted in roles that give them little chance to act. But the movie's main problem is that the protagonist – the dead head – is a bore' (Sayre 1974). One outraged critic even called it 'the greatest film of the thirteenth century' (quoted in Schager 2005). In America, only Jay Cocks and Roger Ebert defended the film. The former considered it 'full of fury and bile … a troubling, idiosyncratic and finally unsuccessful film' (1974). Cocks also suggested that it may be a self-mocking provocation to the director's many critics, a theory explored in-depth in chapter 3. Ebert, one of the first to praise *The Wild Bunch*, called it 'some sort of bizarre masterpiece' and observed that Peckinpah was 'asking us to somehow see past the horror and the blood to the sad poem he's trying to write about the human condition' (2001). The film fared slightly better with critics in the UK. It got a positive review in the *Monthly Film Bulletin* in 1975 (see Thomson 2009) while Chris Petit in *Time Out* praised the film, albeit in a manner that served to warn the unwary:

> There's no suspense; what happens is as predictable as it is inevitable. Peckinpah has structured a slow, almost meditative film out of carefully fashioned images that weave inextricable links between sex, death, music and violence. (1998: 28–9)

Richard Combs in *Sight & Sound* called it 'savagely succesful' (1975: 121) but for Derek Elley in *Films and Filming* 'Peckinpah's grasp of the situation falters as the slow-motion increases … Warren Oates, sad to say, is not yet capable of carrying an entire film … the play with brutality and profanity appears merely childish' (1975: 35). Looking back on the occasion of the film's re-release, the *Observer*'s Philip French recalled how his initial description of the film as 'a combination of Jacobean revenge tragedy, classical quest myth and political fable' that takes place in 'an emblematic Mexico that Lowry, Greene, Lawrence and Traven would recognise' (2009) earned him a place in *Private Eye* magazine's Pseud's Corner.

The film bombed at the box office. It was banned in Sweden and Argentina. UA took out adverts a quarter of the usual size. But marketing a film about a man, a woman and a severed head was always going to present problems. The North American promotional campaign made it look like another thriller in the mould of *The Getaway*. The poster emphasised the violence (with images of bodies falling and Bennie's gun) and Vega's sex appeal (an image of her with her dress hanging off), with the tag-line: 'Was one man's life worth 1 million dollars and the death of 21 men?' For the European release, the marketing made more of the Peckinpah brand name: both the West German and the French posters have the director's name prominently positioned. While the German one uses a familiar image of an unwashed hand clutching the locket containing Al's photo (an image used for US re-releases and on the R1 and R2 DVD sleeves), the French poster is much more striking: a yellow faux-Wanted poster, bearing an image of a bloodied Oates and the memorable tag-line: 'attention! cet homme est dangereux il recherche une tete' ('attention! this man is dangerous, he searches for a head'). The weirdest promotional campaign was that used in Turkey, where the poster shows an illustrated, muscle-bound man who looks nothing like Oates, bursting out of his shirt like the Hulk. He stands astride a decapitated body, holding a bloody machete in one hand and a bleeding severed head in the other, while a woman wearing only a thong lounges decorously in the background.

How do you market a film about a man, a woman and a severed head?

Steven Prince relates a story that demonstrates Peckinpah's fruitless attempts to emphasise the love story in the promotion of his film:

> [Peckinpah] wrote to producer Helmut Dantine that the trailer looked good, but added, 'We should cut down the final shoot-out, in order to accentuate the love theme a little more'. (1998: 149)

One only has to see the trailer to see that Peckinpah didn't get his wish. The emphasis is firmly on action and the anticipation of violence, from Bennie buying his machete and standing in the grave to Quill firing his machine gun, an incredible amount of shooting and slow-motion death.

The trailer's voice-over reinforces this, while also emphasising an unusually strong authorial connection:

> [Over a shot of Bennie, wearing shades] This man will become an animal.
> [Elita in the shower and being stripped by the biker] This woman's dreams of love will be destroyed.
> Innocent people will suffer. 25 people will die. All be-

cause of Alfredo Garcia and only one man really knows why. Sam Peckinpah.

His career never really recovered. Peckinpah had used up all of the critical kudos he had earned with *The Wild Bunch* and although he would have commercial hits (such as *The Killer Elite*) and some good reviews (for *Cross of Iron*), he was in a downward spiral both professionally and personally. Between 1975 and his death in 1984, there was cocaine, paranoia, a heart attack and a couple of videos for Julian Lennon ('Do you know', he said to his second wife, Begonia Palacios, days before his death, 'the last film I made was five minutes long?' (quoted in Fine 2005: 376)). But he remained defiantly proud of *Alfredo Garcia*. When asked, late in life, whether he harboured any desires to make a 'pure Peckinpah', he answered 'I did *Alfredo Garcia* and did it exactly the way I wanted to. Good or bad, like it or not. That was my film' (Weddle 1994: 497).

2

'THERE'S NOTHING SACRED ABOUT A HOLE IN THE GROUND OR THE MAN THAT'S IN IT. OR YOU. OR ME': *ALFREDO GARCIA*'S REPUTATION

POSTHUMOUS PECKINPAH

Peckinpah's reputation has grown considerably since his death in 1984. Indeed, in 2005, Leland Poague stated that, unlike contemporaries such as Polanski, Penn and Altman, 'Peckinpah's devotees are many, comprising an ad hoc army of loyal outlaws and garrulous misfits dwelling on the frontiers of academic film study' (2005). In addition to David Weddle's exhaustive biography *"If They Move…Kill 'Em!" The Life and Times of Sam Peckinpah* (1994), there have been a number of books published on the man and his work. A glance at some of these titles offers a good insight into the nature of Peckinpah's cinema: *Crucified Heroes, Bloody Sam, Savage Cinema: Sam Peckinpah and the Rise of Ultra-Violent Cinema, Passion & Poetry, This Wounded Cinema, This Wounded*

Life: Violence and Utopia in the Films of Sam Peckinpah. In addition, there are a number of documentary features focusing on his life and work, including *Sam Peckinpah: Man of Iron* (Paul Joyce, 1992), *Sam Peckinpah's West: Legacy of a Hollywood Renegade*, and *Passion and Poetry: The Ballad of Sam Peckinpah* (Mike Siegel, 2005). There are also a number of unrelated films dedicated to the Old Sand Crab: *Killer: A Journal of Murder* (Tim Metcalfe, 1996), the bizarre *Running Scared* (Wayne Kramer, 2006) and *Death Proof* (2007), Quentin Tarantino's half of the *Grindhouse* double feature, which contains some explicit references to Peckinpah's work.

Moviedrome (1988–2000) was the BBC2 series of cult movies, which has attained a cult following of its own in recent years: see the video-taped introductions to the show on YouTube and the number of websites that offer both nostalgic reminiscences and gratitude (such as a description of the show as 'an extraordinary defence of sorts against the ugly, powerful and very ordinary hold of school' and its 'mission to educate a generation about the joys of lost or forgotten or once-derided films' (Collings 2008)). The show's first presenter was the filmmaker Alex Cox (who had offered his own scrappy homage to Peckinpah and Sergio Leone with *Straight To Hell* (1987)). In 1994, *Alfredo Garcia* was screened as part of a Peckinpah double bill (with *Major Dundee*). In his introduction, Cox confessed to an initial disappointment with Peckinpah's film, seeing it as a let-down after the high of *The Wild Bunch*. However, in a journey familiar to many (including this writer), his opinion had changed over time.

This ongoing reassessment has led some to regard *Alfredo Garcia* as a major work, situated somewhere between his acknowledged artistic successes (such as *The Wild Bunch* and *Straw Dogs*) and the underwhelming inconsistency of his later films (*Convoy* and *The Osterman Weekend* (1983)).

It is also worth considering the substantial cult that has sprung up around the star of the film, Warren Oates. He has been the subject of a documentary feature (the above-mentioned *Across the Border*) as well as a number of websites dedicated to the man and his films (the best-known being Warren Oates at tedstrong.com). In an essay about the actor, Melissa Holbrook Pierson talks of missing the man and 'also missing the movies that made Oates what he became, the kind that are painted with a million shades of grey. It's the kind of loss you never get over' (1999). For Richard Luck, Oates was a creature of his turbulent times, a kind of Henry Fonda for the cynical, violent 1970s:

> the effects of corruption and double-cross were writ large in the leer, filthy mane and craven eyes of Warren Oates ... As a thug or a bully, cowhand or hired gun, bank robber or cockfighter, Warren Oates gave the American movie-going public a chance to look at itself, to see what it had become in the years between Korea and Grenada. (2000)

There is even, somewhat incongruously, a MySpace site in his name, where we learn that he has 379 friends, his star-sign is Cancer, he'd like to meet 'any other deceased character actors or anyone willing to buy me a drink' and his interests include 'cross-country road trips with disembodied heads'.

Peckinpah, too, is on MySpace with a number of other dead auteurs among his friends including Fritz Lang, Yasujiró Ozu and Rainer Werner Fassbinder, while on Facebook, the director has 4,851 fans. These posthumous appearances on popular social networking sites point to the cult appeal of certain dead celebrities while also serving to unite a global community of fans. The fact that both the director and actor died young further boosts that cult appeal, an appeal in no way diminished by the perceived 'outlaw status' of these hard-drinking, grizzled men.

It is not too much of a stretch to regard *Alfredo Garcia* as a 'cursed film', the term coined by filmmaker, author and satanist, Kenneth Anger, to describe 'films that feature stars who died soon after production was completed' (Brottman 2008). Oates, Peckinpah, Gig Young and Jerry Fielding would all be dead within ten years of making this film, which is so suffused with death. Mikita Brottman also considers the fascination Anger and legions of cult fans have with 'films involving one or more celebrities who took their own lives, all of which have come to attain an odd kind of cult status of their own' (2008). She considers the 'chicken-run' car race in *Rebel Without a Cause* (Nicholas Ray, 1955) in the light of James Dean's fatal 1955 crash but Gig Young's performance as Sappensly is an even better example: it is impossible to ignore the eerie parallels between his role as a gun-toting misogynist killer and his final, real-life role as murderer and suicide.

Like a lot of cult movies (*The Night of the Hunter* (Charles Laughton, 1958), *Performance* (Donald Cammell/Nicolas Roeg, 1970), *The Wicker Man* (Robin Hardy, 1973)), the very qualities that led to the film's initial failure are the ones that underpin its cult reputation. In the case of *Alfredo Garcia*, what critics saw as incompetence is now regarded by some as integrity. What could once be dismissed as self-indulgence can now be seen as a kind of demented autobiography. Indeed, it's the scrappy inconsistency of Peckinpah's film that, for aficionados, raises it above his other, not inconsiderable, cinematic achievements. This 'low-fi', dogged quality and the relentless nihilism of the thing make it seem untrammeled and uncompromising, in a way that has become familiar in the decades since (*Taxi Driver* (Martin Scorsese, 1975), punk, the New Queer Cinema, the films of Abel Ferrara). Indeed, one can argue that without *Alfredo Garcia*, there would be no *Wild at Heart* (David Lynch, 1990), no *Pulp Fiction* (Quentin Tarantino, 1994), no *Dead Man* (Jim Jarmusch, 1996). It also has the cult appeal of a number of other works by noted directors that were either overlooked or scorned upon their release, such as *Peeping Tom* (Michael Powell, 1960), *Buffalo Bill and the Indians* (Robert Altman, 1976), *Eureka* (Nicolas Roeg, 1982), *King of Comedy* (Martin Scorsese, 1983). Indeed, David Weddle has suggested that the film could be regarded as 'a cult within a cult' (1994: 498), referring to its unique status in the oeuvre of this most divisive of directors. The Internet database Rotten Tomatoes, where English-language film reviews are compiled, gives *Alfredo Garcia* a 'Fresh Tomato Rating' of 80%, reflecting this shift in critical thinking. However, even some of the positive responses will sound off-putting to many: 'trashy' (Delapa 2004), 'bleak, purposely revolting and unsentimental' (Schager 2005), 'so much death and spiritual poison' (Prince 1995: 151). Or how about *Entertainment Weekly*'s 'not much of a plot ... You feel like you need a delousing after watching Oates slowly lose his mind' (Nashawaty 2006)? For Terence Butler, the film 'has the strange distinction of being the worst directed of great American movies' (1979: 9). The *Third Virgin Film Guide* regards the film as one of the director's 'more daring films' and 'one of cinema's more perversely intriguing experiences' but also acknowledges the 'sloppy photography, a few unintentionally humorous scenes and an excess of Peckinpah's signature slow-motion violence' (Pallot *et al.* 1994: 102–3). Michael Atkinson in the *Village Voice* has looked back at the film twice in recent years, on both occasions offering evocative descriptions: it is 'a rough-hewn black box of metaphors and existential funk you can never finish unpacking' (2000) and 'a violent hope-deprived neo-noir that even the Nixon era couldn't handle' from 'the underworld demon king of masculine genre angst and the world's first genuine action craftsman' (2005). For Rick Moody, 'there's a desperation' to the film although he acknowledges that 'it is hard to turn away from it. Train wrecks, after all, offer a visceral satisfaction, if only for their scale' (2009). Critic Elvis Mitchell, in *Sam Peckinpah's West*, suggested that the film should be called 'Bring Me the Diseased Soul of Sam Peckinpah', while Phil Nugent suggests 'it gives you a one-of-a-kind heady rush taking the popular idea of not giving a fuck as far as it can go – farther than most people who claim to be attracted to the idea of not giving a fuck would ever dream of going' (2005).

It is surely fitting that a film as boozy and ramshackle as *Alfredo Garcia* has no staged events or conventions *a la The Rocky Horror Picture Show* (Jim Sharman, 1975). It seems perverse to get together and celebrate such a bleak vision of dust and death. It is also by no means rehabilitated, unlike many other 'problematic' films, such as *Freaks* (Tod Browning, 1933), *The Night of the Hunter* or *Performance*, that have now taken their place in 'the canon'. It remains a film that thrills, provokes and bores in equal measure, lionised on obscure websites and referenced by obsessive fans, artists and poets, those whom Leland Poague called 'outlaws and misfits'.

And always that title. It provides a running joke on the Radio 4 panel game, *I'm Sorry I Haven't A Clue* (1972–present), inspired the title of pap such as the lame Brit-com *Bring Me the Head of Mavis Davis* (John Henderson, 1997) and the television show *Bring Me the Head of Light Entertainment* (1997).

In recent years, a number of critics have challenged the conventional notion that Peckinpah went into terminal decline after *Pat Garrett and Billy the Kid*: Mark Crispin Miller, Steven Prince and Gabrielle Murray have all written persuasive defences of late Peckinpah in general and *Alfredo Garcia* in particular. Paul Seydor called it 'the grimmest, the bleakest, the funniest, and the most horrifying of his films. People will look back on us and wonder how we failed to understand *Alfredo Garcia*' (in Weddle 1994: 498).

However, this revisionist view is not one shared by everyone and a number of critics still seem to regard the film as the point at which Peckinpah came undone. Gene Shalit, when asked by *Time* magazine to name the worst film he had ever seen, suggested the Pauly Shore comedy *Encino Man* (Les Mayfield, 1992) or *Bring Me the Head of Alfredo Garcia*, adding 'I had to go to the emergency room after each one' (in Orecklin 1998). *Halliwell's Film & Video Guide* calls it a 'gruesome, sickly action melodrama with revolting detail: the nadir of a director obsessed with violence' (in Walker 2001:114). *Leonard Maltin's Movie and Video Guide 1999* considers it 'a sub-par bloodbath [which] doesn't even have the usual Peckinpah fast pace' (1998: 175). Even Weddle seems ambivalent about the film. In his biography of Peckinpah, he acknowledges the growing cult around *Alfredo Garcia* but doesn't seem to belong to it himself: he devotes seventy pages to the making and reception of *The Wild Bunch* and six-and-a-half to *Alfredo Garcia* (in a chapter titled, appropriately enough, 'Into the Abyss'; see 1994: 307–77, 492–8). Interviewed for *Sam Peckinpah's West*, he suggests that the film 'seems to sail way beyond definitions of good or bad, [it's] a genuine work of art, a completely demented movie'.

In January 2009, the film was given a limited theatrical re-release in the UK, the centrepiece of a BFI Peckinpah retrospective. This time, the reviews were largely positive, although tempered with characteristic ambivalence, possibly as a result of the film's growing cult reputation. John Patterson in the *Guardian*, for example, talks of 'the narrative slackness … lazily directed scenes and no shortage of evidence that Peckinpah just didn't care anymore' while acknowledging that 'the film's power is undeniable: stark, nihilistic, overbearingly macho and undeniably misogynistic' (2008). Edward Porter in the *Sunday Times* states that it combines 'maudlin, drunken self-pity' with 'all the sleazy virtues of a good 1970s exploitation flick' (2009), while in its sister paper, the *Times*, long-time Peckinpah admirer Kim Newman dubs it 'the essence of cinematic pulp … a ragged, not-for-everyone masterpiece' (2009). *Electric Sheep* magazine summed it up as 'like Peckinpah himself, a mixture of the very, very good and the very, very bad' (Long 2009) while for Nigel Andrews in the *Financial Times*, it 'makes Peckinpah's early benchmark essay in violence, *The Wild Bunch*, look like a mild stroll in an abbatoir' (2009).

ALFREDO ONLINE

The Internet is a boon to those studying film reception, making, as Mike Chopra-Gant suggests 'fans' activities and discussions … more available for analysis' (2008: 19), allowing 'fans across the world to communicate with each other' (Jancovich *et al.* 2003: 4) as part of 'a large niche audience' (ibid.) The fan-sites and talk boards that proliferate on the web offer, for the first time, access to a wide range of opinions, hyperbole, bile and bad grammar, in large part due to the (relative) lack of gatekeepers and tastemakers found in the 'traditional' media. However, there is some equivocation about the way new technologies such as the Internet affect cult fandom. For Mark Jancovich *et al.*, the web 'threatens the sense of distinction and exclusivity … on which cult movie fandom depends, and threatens to blur the very distinctions that organise it' (2003: 4) while for Michael Z. Newman, the easy access to films offered by video, DVD and the Internet 'makes the cult mode of film experience much more typical, more available to more viewers', rendering that which was once marginal 'more of a mainstream practice' (2008). Writing about the role played by the Internet in promoting *The Blair*

Witch Project (Daniel Myrick/Eduardo Sanchez, 1999), J. P. Telotte discusses Paul Virilio and his notion of 'glocalization', wherein 'the electronic experience ... with its tendency to bring together many and different places ... also leaves us without a real place – decentred and lost' (2003: 272).

There is, of course, a considerable irony about Peckinpah's presence on the web. His films are full of a hatred for the new: the director once stated that he detested machines: 'The problem started when they discovered the wheel' (quoted in Seydor 1980: 250). Think of the way the automobile is used as a torture device in *The Wild Bunch*, or the way it puts Cable Hogue first out of business and then in the ground. Consider the wacky satire of television and the surveillance society in *The Osterman Weekend*. This hatred of all things new went way beyond the Luddite: Peckinpah frequently presents children as possessors of a lack of innocence bordering on the malign: burning the scorpion and ants in *The Wild Bunch*, swinging on the hangman's noose in *Pat Garrett and Billy the Kid* and, in *Alfredo Garcia*, flocking round the bounty-hunters who buy them ice cream, picking up the gun next to El Jefe's corpse and watching blankly as the guards pump bullets into Bennie.

The large amount of online material on *Alfredo Garcia* is illuminating, partly in the way it highlights a disconnect between print media and web resources. The Internet material is almost exclusively provided by men, unlike the published work by writers including Kathleen Murphy, Pauline Kael and Gabrielle Murray. It is also frequently aggressively partisan, emphasising the 'purity' of Peckinpah's film over the work of other, more celebrated directors while rejecting textual analysis in favour of evocative analogies (tomatoes, toothache and, unsurprisingly, booze). But, as in the case of the mainstream media, the film retains its ability to provoke, upset, bore and ultimately divide audiences.

The Internet Movie Database (IMDb) is a good indicator
as to both to the enduring appeal of Peckinpah's film and its
aforementioned divisive nature. At the time of writing (summer 2008), there are 81 user reviews. Some are glowing: 'it
sits at the same table as the greats, perhaps across the way
from *Citizen Kane* or *Raging Bull*' (sothisislife, Southern CA);
some are damning: 'I haven't been able to make it all the
way through, but its been a painful experience so far. I'll bet
that most people seeing this movie won't make it past the
first half hour. Its [sic] that unwatchable' (eman6101, USA);
some are off-beat: 'reminds me of biting into a ripe tomato
– messy and intensely satisfying (if you like tomatoes)' (Jason
Forestein, Somerville, MA). Taken as a whole, these comments offer a useful glimpse into the aforementioned mind-
set of the online cult film audience: passionate, aggressive,
committed and insulting. Other directors (Paul Verhoeven,
Oliver Stone, Quentin Tarantino, Joel and Ethan Coen, Robert
Rodriguez) are compared to Peckinpah and found wanting.
Some of the descriptions are poetic: 'the screen practically
sweats' (Flixer1957, Columbia County, NY); 'This movie flat-
tened me. Desperation and flies, lots of flies' (sinistre1111,
Kasparhauser, NJ); 'this scuzzy, squirrelly road movie looks
less like self-parody than self-autopsy … Each cut is like a dy-
ing man's blink' (Superfly-13). Peckinpah is compared to Jean
Cocteau (mikenuell, El Dorado, USA) and Shakespeare (KFL,
Bloomington, IN).

Some of the users seem to take what they perceive as
the film's shortcomings personally: 'beware, this film is slow,
boring and at times just plain stupid. I'm surprised that there
are so many scholars and authors out there who examine
each Peckinpah film in such in-depth detail when the film is
just plain bad and has no cinematic quality to it whatsoever'
(James_Bond_007_218, Wellington, New Zealand); 'Only for
people who think they see things in movies other [sic] don't

or provide subtext and symbolism which they pretend the director intended to show to satisfy their elitist egos. I am a director too. Cinema is visual. Directors don't try to hide things. We are subtle but not evasive. I hate this movie and I loved Convoy' (Raskimono). The cult movie audience is often regarded as a boy's club and this, when combined with the 'macho' tag that is often attached to Peckinpah's films, leads to Isela Vega being frequently judged on her appearance, far more than any of the male performers: 'Isela Vegas [sic] playing the female lead, added only two things to the film: her breasts, which she wasn't shy about showing' (ccthemovie-man-1, Lockport, NY); 'a [sic] aging, crab infested girl friend' (manchesteruk, Manchester, UK); 'the choice of a looking-next-door-girl [sic] [Vega] to play a professional prostitute is a flaw of the movie' (pzanardo, Padova, Italy). The talk boards of the IMDb have seven pages of comments on the film, from discussions of DVD aspect ratios to repeated questions about Bennie's/Sam's glasses: 'where can I get sunglasses like those in the film?' (pr0fessional@hotmail.com) and 'what kind of sunglasses was Warren Oates wearing?' (Nostalgiadrag).

The boards also, unsurprisingly, spend a lot of time arguing the merits of this still-contentious film. It is described as 'a masterpiece' (narliecharlie) and 'a boring piece of shit movie' (who_wants_a_pony); 'the ultimate Sam Peckinpah film' (teejay6682) and 'the worst film ever made' (Mar-cinema). There are also posts on subjects ranging from costume (gigyoung11 notes how 'Benny [sic] accidentally pulls off his clip-on tie when tucking away the fronted money into his off-the-rack-leisure jacket') to Isela Vega (deleted user asks 'anyone else think the girl was beautiful?') and that nemesis of Peckinpah admirers, Michael Medved ('a prissy, obnoxious, self-righteous asshole' according to Irving-Joey while to kimberleymhn, he's 'a joke'). Self-explanatory threads include 'Was Alfredo Garcia really the baby's father?' (clive-ihd);

'CINEMA PSYCHOSIS' (uscmd); 'were Quill and his partner gay?' (will the redneck); and 'Greatest Drinking Movie Of All Time' (originaltbyrd).

It's much the same story on the Amazon website. Out of eleven user reviews, five like the film, six don't. As is par for the course, even some of the positive reviews sound like bad ones: 'Best enjoyed with a bottle of Jack Daniels … the grimmest vision of humanity ever created' (Stephen B. Hughes, Merrimac, USA, 12/08/2003); 'an alcoholic suicide note found in a sleazy motel bed … It will not make you feel good' (Eric Krupin, Salt Lake City, Utah, 01/03/01); 'you may feel a little queasy placing this video on your shelf alongside your Lawrence of Arabias or your Seventh Seals. It is not only not a classic (and will never be one), it is informed by one of the most disgusting visions of life since Sade … A black, bitter movie to be savored late at night with the poison and people of your own choosing' (A Viewer, 3/07/2000). There are unqualified raves, however: 'My favorite Peckinpah film. Yeah, you heard me right. This is the one where we can clearly perceive Sam flying of [sic] the deep end, and yet it is still some kind of graceful ugly crazy masterpiece' (newmanmonster999, Berkeley, CA, USA, 20/02/2006); 'This is a brilliant & riveting movie with terrific acting, terrific pace, terrific ending, terrific everything … as real as a toothache or a dying best friend … There are so many amazing layers & textures & details in this great film, you'll watch it many times, believe me' (inframan, the lower depths, 16/10/2005).

The bad reviews, however, are really bad, most of them every bit as vitriolic as the critical response that initially greeted the film: 'Easily Peckinpah's worst film and one of the worst American movies of the seventies. It marked the beginning of the director's decline into booze-and-drug self-absorption from which he never emerged' (A Viewer, 3/05/2004); 'It's been 30 years since I've seen this film on cable. I decided to re-visit this obscure film and see if I missed anything in the initial viewing. As it turned out, I didn't miss anything ... It's also a long, tedious film that is not one of his best' (smooth-jazzandmore, Clay, NY, USA, 29/01/2007); 'It totally failed my expectations ... What I got was a farce. The plot is basic and uninteresting, no real hooks and horrible characterization. What a joke of a plot. I think Peckinpah just wanted an excuse to throw in as much violence as possible, albeit violence which has no cause, rhyme or reason' (Garth, Columbus, OH, 9/01/2006); 'This movie is BAD. Very, very BAD. It's like real life: long, boring, and pointless. I wish I could find something nice to say about it, but ... Geez, is it dull ... It's just a bunch of mean, ugly people doing mean, ugly things to each other. Pointless. Dumb characters. Dumb story. Dumb climax. Dumb movie' (Mojo Jojo 26/12/2006); 'As bad as the title sounds. Very bad photography, acting, cheap nudity and dialogue with plenty of bad effects of shootings and killings. I sure can say that this is one of the worst movies I have seen in a very long time' (W. Noshie, 15/12/2005); 'Possibly the worst film ever made. This film was made when Peckinpah was stoned while on the set most of the time, and it shows ... Basically, this film is a waste of the viewers' time, as all Peckinpah spends his time doing is figuring out different ways to disrobe the female lead. Forget the plot, as there really isn't one. Suffice to say, if you watch this film, you'll see why Peckinpah had the final cut taken away from him on all his other films. BTW, the only reason I give this film one star is that it's the lowest I could go' (M. Fisher, Yukon, Oklahoma, USA, 3/12/2005).

Even self-confessed aficionados of cult films demonstrate considerable ambivalence towards Peckinpah's film. On the Internet discussion forum alt.cult-movies, one poster says 'I watched this film again the other night for about the fifth time and I still dont [sic] know whether it is a good movie or not ...

some of the film just doesn't make sense (mnbc6jeh, 1996), while another agrees: 'I don't know whether I like it or not either. It works very well on a technical level and it does have a nice plot line, but its [sic] just a bit difficult to watch and very hard to truly understand' (D. Fresko, 1996). Other posters describe it as 'bleak. That's the word, bleak' (Mary Virginia Burke, 1998) , having the 'best "omigod, I want out" feel this side of Italiozombie flicks ... Existential subtext to spare' (Christopher M. Stangl, 1998) and being 'very very seedy. If you prefer your cinema violent and ugly then this is your cup of tea' (Karl Lyons, 1998).

There are dozens of reviews on film websites and they are almost uniformly positive, reflecting both the ongoing critical re-evaluation of the film and the fact that a large number of film e-zines and fan-sites celebrate the off-beat, the cult and the non-mainstream: witness, for example, the Abel Ferrara Virtual Library, at least four Harmony Korine fan-sites and a fan-site for and numerous interviews with Monte Hellman, all figures not particularly well-served by traditional print media. While these specialised reviewers often take great pains to contextualise Peckinpah's film, invoking such disparate figures as Lyndon Johnson, Brian De Palma and Jesus Christ, their comments are no less impassioned or impressionistic. It is striking how, like the user comments quoted above, so many of these writers resort to visceral imagery: shit, pain, grime, sleaze.

There are *Alfredo Garcia* pieces on a number of evocatively-titled sites: for *Not Coming to a Cinema Near You*, it is 'a graphic spin on the road movie ... we're also given a strong study in the workings of a human mind' (Balz 2006), while *Crushed by Inertia* considers it:

the work of a special visionary director ... Shit is just coming at you, and what makes you a man is how you decide to deal with it. Not the most complicated idea in the world but then, when you make a movie as brisk, entertaining and daring as *Alfredo Garcia*, even the simplest idea can seem mesmerizing. (Lons 2005)

At *The 70s Movies Rewind*, Peckinpah's film shares space with such disparate fare as *Blackenstein* (William A. Levey, 1973), *Barry Lyndon* (Stanley Kubrick, 1974) and *The Muppet Movie* (James Frawley, 1979) and is vividly described as:

probably one of the most vicious, brutal and unsentimental films ever made ... teeming with angst, overflowing with rage ... an exercise in absolute, unadulterated nihilism ... Yet in this mire of pain, faded dreams and a severed head clouded in flies is an underlying beauty in this film. (Fitzgerald 2003)

Combustible Celluloid calls it 'dreamy, dreary ... one of the director's best ... Oates' antihero is among the loneliest men in the cinema, and one of its greatest performances' (Anderson 2005), while for LazyBastard.com it is 'sweet, sweet, sweet ... bizarre, beautiful and savage. Comparing the film to an imaginary film noir collaboration between David Goodis and Charles Bukowski and Oates to 'Tom Waits at his booziest', Jeff Lester concludes 'you couldn't have paid me to hang around Peckinpah while he was alive but I sure wish there was someone around who could make 'em like this' (1998). *This Savage Art* has a Sam Peckinpah blog-a-thon and their piece on *Alfredo Garcia* is good on the fan response, undoubtedly hyperbolic (casting the director as a kind of Christ figure, no less) but also sincere: 'I don't think there is another director living or dead who actually personified every frame of the films they directed. He was a Hollywood legend and he suffered both physically and mentally because of it. It didn't matter, what was on the screen was everything. That is with us forever' (Speruzzi 2007). *The Spinning Image* emphasises the ambivalent response to the film, calling it 'obsessively sleazy … the action moves at a snail's pace' and concluding 'it's a wild-eyed, staggering ramble of bloodshed; some have found bleak, grimy poetry in the film, but the presentation is so unfriendly that only Peckinpah true believers need apply' (Clark 2008). On *The High Hat*, Phil Nugent borrows a striking analogy from a former US President:

> Lyndon Johnson once said that 'when you have a moth-er-in-law, and that mother-in-law has only one eye, and that eye is in the centre of her forehead, you don't keep her in the living room.' The mother-in-law that LBJ had in mind was Vietnam; Sam Peckinpah's was *Bring Me the Head of Alfredo Garcia*, the labour of love that he directed, conceived and co-wrote, and saw released in 1974 to empty theatres and general revulsion. (2005)

There is also a lengthy article on the film by Stephen Boone on the blog *Big Media Vandalism*, which is significant for the way it seeks to reclaim the film for what it calls 'minority filmmak-ers'. Describing it as 'the saddest, strangest hood movie ever made', Boone suggests that while *Scarface* (Brian De Palma, 1983) is a recurring motif in the work of many hip-hop artists and filmmakers, it 'hasn't a tenth as much to say about the fes-tering (North) American dream as *Alfredo Garcia*'. He considers the representation of women and Mexico, describing the film as an 'unintentional time capsule full of lessons for future gen-erations of genre-loving, nihilism-baiting underclass auteurs'. His case for the film's relevance is worth quoting in full:

> *Bring Me the Head of Alfredo Garcia* offers young ur-ban filmmakers torn between exhilarating *Scarface/*

Grand Theft Auto-style genre nihilism and *Boyz N the Hood* sentimentality a different way to approach the reality of the streets, the housing project, the jailhouse. The Peckinpah road map avoids boredom and pretension without sacrificing humanism and true feeling. Call him the deadbeat dad of a hybrid pulp/art ghetto cinema that never was, or has yet to be. (2005)

YouTube, the video-sharing site, contains a number of Peckinpah-related clips, some official (film clips, trailers) and some amateur, made by fans. These clips offer fans a chance to 'personalise' a favourite film: sometimes re-editing and re-scoring it in much the same way as authors of 'slash fiction' have done in print for years. At the time of writing (October 2008), visitors to the site can see the trailer, the opening, the gun battle with the Garcia family, the shoot-out at the hotel and the end of the film. One can even watch the film, downloading it in ten-minute segments. There is also a homemade music video featuring clips from Peckinpah films including *Alfredo Garcia*, set (somewhat incongruously) to the music of Linkin Park.

The impenetrable (at least to this writer) net-based educational art project, Cosmic Baseball Association, have based a virtual game on *Alfredo Garcia*, setting characters against actors. The website reports that the game 'was devoid of violence, misogyny, and nihilism, all words used to describe the film'. The game notes report that the actors won and concludes that 'No doubt the romance with Peckinpah will continue' (2007). Just as Peckinpah's film is often considered to have poetic aspirations, so, conversely, we can find poetry that aspires to Peckinpah's film: 'What we need in american [sic] poetry is a poet who can bring us the rotting head of Alfredo Garcia which is really the rotting head of american [sic] poetry covered with all of its stink and all of its scum and all of its shit. Someone who can bring back the rotting head of american [sic] poetry so that it can receive a decent burial'. That is Todd Moore from his 2006 Outlaw Poetry page. It comes as no surprise that the divisive nature of *Alfredo Garcia* even affects outlaw poets, as Karl Koweski's posted reply demonstrates: 'Sam Peckinpah hated people and his raging ego didn't allow him to collaborate with people very long. And Bennie was machine-gunned to death shortly after delivering Alfredo Garcia's head' (2006). The *Fauxhunter* site, set up to expose Internet scams, was set up by an Alfredo Garcia: 'my father was called Garcia and he thought it was a good joke to name me from [sic] a dumb movie that I haven't even seen yet but everyone keeps shouting 'bring me the head of Alfredo Garcia' at me. Haha' (2004–06).

Like Alfredo, Peckinpah's film refuses to stay buried.

3

'DON'T LOOK AT ME WITH THOSE GODDAMN FUCKIN' EYES': ALCOHOL CINEMA

STORY

If the narrative of *Bring Me the Head of Alfredo Garcia* is a muddle, the story has the simplicity and power of myth. El Jefe, a wealthy Mexican rancher, puts a price on the head of the man who impregnated then abandoned his daughter. When two bounty-hunters turn up at a bar-cum-brothel in Mexico City in search of their quarry and question Bennie, the drunken piano player, he sees his chance to get rich. He embarks on a quest to find the wanted man, taking along his girlfriend, Elita, a singer and part-time whore who, he discovers, cuckolded him with Alfredo. She tells Bennie that Alfredo is dead but, to her horror, he decides to try and collect the bounty anyway. When they decide to camp out after a tyre blow-out, they are set upon by a couple of bikers, one of whom tries to rape Elita only to have her respond passionately. Bennie kills both men and despite Elita's pleas that they give up, he insists they continue. In a rural cemetery,

Bennie digs up the body but he is ambushed and buried alive with the murdered Elita. When Bennie rises from the grave, leaving Elita with the decapitated body of her ex-lover, he is a man transformed. After much killing, including the deaths of the Garcia family and the two bounty-hunters, he gets the head back. Now more interested in killing than money, he slaughters El Jefe's hoods in their hotel room and finds a note in the pocket of a corpse that leads him to El Jefe. Bennie travels to El Jefe's compound to deliver the head before pulling his gun and, at the urging of the patriarch's daughter, killing El Jefe. Attempting to flee with the money and the head, Bennie is shot and killed. This tale of greed, murder and madness south of the border consciously echoes John Huston's classic *The Treasure of the Sierra Madre* (1948). Peckinpah was a great admirer of Huston ('compared to Huston, I'm still in seventh grade' (Murray 2008: 113)) and both films concern themselves with gringo loser anti-heroes seeking their fortune in Mexico. In case we missed this, the connection is made clear when Gig Young's bounty-hunter gives his name as Fred C. Dobbs, the name of the Humphrey Bogart character in Huston's film. In a sense, he is Dobbs and so is Bennie: as a bandido says to Bogart in the earlier film: 'I know you. You're the guy in the hole.' This is a world where everyone is Dobbs, the guy in the hole, on the make, soulless, grasping and crazed with greed.

Indeed, it is useful to consider Roger Ebert's description of *The Treasure of the Sierra Madre* as 'a film about a seedy loser driven mad by greed' (2003) or Louis B. Mayer's thoughts on the same director's *The Asphalt Jungle* (1950): 'full of nasty, ugly people doing nasty, ugly things' (quoted in Grobel 1989: 336). Both men could be talking about Peckinpah's film. But the execution of *The Treasure of the Sierra Madre* and *Alfredo Garcia* differ wildly. Whereas the earlier film is a model of clarity and economy, Peckinpah sacrifices these things and replaces them with a tone which is often uncertain, a streak of black humour that may or may not be intentional and a mood that lurches from the revolting to the poetic and back again. Gabrielle Murray's description of the film's 'strange complexity and haunting lyricism' (2002) is a good one. Maybe the best example of the film's sick poetry is when Bennie is driving away from the gun battle with the Garcia family. Muddy from the grave, bleeding from a shovel to the head, he drives his battered car, waving away the stink of rotting flesh, talking to the head over the buzzing of flies. 'You got jewels in your ears, diamonds up your nose', he tells it (him? I'm reminded of *The Tenant* (Roman Polanski, 1976) here, with Polanski's Trelkovsky musing, 'If you cut off my head, what do I say: me and my head or me and my body?'). Bennie's talking to the head may well be another nod to *The Treasure of the Sierra Madre*, wherein the increasingly unhinged Dobbs talks to himself as the vintage prospector Howard (Walter Huston) tells him, 'It's a bad sign when a fella starts talking to himself'. Or to a severed head in a sack.

It is this scrappy quality, the longueurs and the choppy editing that help to give the film its unique power. In his previous films, Peckinpah had shown himself to be a master of pacing and tone. This can be seen in both the oppressive tension of *Straw Dogs* and the stoned elegy that is *Pat Garrett and Billy the Kid*. But *Alfredo Garcia* does away with both of those approaches, giving us instead a loose, rambling structure that has a grim, hypnotic pull all of its own. It often seems like two films stitched together. The first is a slow-moving, often uncertain love story with meandering stretches and moments so intense they are hard to watch. The second is a faster, violent neo-western, with splashes of gothic excess and pitch-black humour. This duality has the effect, when combined with the distancing devices the director frequently uses, such as slow-motion and a bewildering number of cuts, of creating a sense of disorientation in the viewer. It's hard to say how intentional this is. As mentioned, many critics feel *Alfredo Garcia* is the point at which a talented filmmaker lost the plot, never to get it back, while others consider its weird, alienating effects and tonal shifts to be part of a strategy: Steven Prince talks of the film's 'prolonged assault on the normative pleasures viewers look for in narrative cinema' (1998: 151) while, for Terence Butler, 'despite the diffuseness of its dream-like setting, *Alfredo Garcia* succinctly exposes contradictions underlying Peckinpah's work and the American Dream' (1979: 92).

AUTOBIOGRAPHY: DRINK AND DISAPPOINTMENT

Strategic device or not, the disorientation on show may well have been Peckinpah's. The director's perception of himself as a failure, his seemingly-bottomless well of self-pity and his alcoholism are all important elements in understanding the film. His drinking had long been the stuff of legend but after the *Pat Garrett and Billy the Kid* debacle, it became even more of a problem and he was having regular alcohol-induced blackouts and wild rages. Whenever he stopped, he would smoke a lot of dope. But the drink, the dope, the pills and, from *The Killer Elite* on, the coke aren't simply important as the stuff of anecdote: rather, I think they had a marked effect on Peckinpah's work as well as his personality, and *Alfredo Garcia* is the point in his career when he was starting to unravel, putting this up on the screen for all to see. Certainly, he often invites this confusion between art and artist: in the documentary feature *Passion and Poetry*, the director says, 'all my guts, all my life, everything I am is up there on the screen. It's all there, everything I am is right there.' Peckinpah's drinking has to, I think, be regarded as something inextricably bound up with this film, in much the same way as Hitchcock's sexual kinks inform *Vertigo* (1958) and *Marnie* (1964). The alcohol fuelled two, seemingly contradictory, aspects of his personality that frequently found their way onto the screen: his self-pity and his macho braggadocio. The same duality is also found in John Huston, another legendary drinker, whose films are defined by bluff, macho heroes who talk big but end up engaged in hopeless causes. When Peckinpah says 'a drunk has dreams, a sober man doesn't' (in Bryson 2008: 138), he is not only talking about himself but his alter ego Bennie. Likewise, the director's glib comment to an interviewer: 'would you like to know what I really believe? I believe I'll have another drink' (in Jenson 2008: 78). Rick Moody suggests that *Alfredo Garcia*, with its 'garishness, the half-heartedness of the production values, the fuzzy story and fuzzier characters reminds us that … Peckinpah is among the undisputed poets of alcoholic cinema' (2009). For *Modern Drunkard* magazine ('standing up for your right to get falling down drunk since 1996'), the director is 'an exemplary drunkard … who knew alcohol. He spoke its language' (English 2006). Bennie is sentimental and violent, paranoid and inarticulate, unwashed and unpredictable, a far cry from the pisshead poets of *Barfly* (Barbet Schroeder, 1987), *Leaving Las Vegas* (Mike Figgis, 1985) and *A Love Song for Bobbie Long* (Shainee Gabel, 2004).

Early on, Bennie is dismissed as 'a loser' and he responds with 'nobody loses all the time'. But the black joke at the heart of this film is 'yes, Bennie. Some people do and you are one of them.' Or are we supposed to regard his shooting of El Jefe as a kind of victory? Is Bennie growing and learning, in a kind of bitter parody of the kind of character arc we see so often in mainstream cinema? His words near the end of the film suggest that might be the case: 'I coulda died in Mexico City or T. J. and never known what it was all about.' When we first see him, singing 'Guantanamera' for a bunch of tourists, he bids them farewell by suggesting they go out and 'find the soul of Mexico'. Is this what Bennie does in the end? Does he achieve a sort of enlightenment through all that killing? In interviews to promote the film, Peckinpah describes *Alfredo Garcia* in just such redemptive terms, calling it 'a little picture about human dignity' (quoted in Prince 1998: 146) and suggesting, 'finally, finally, somebody gets pissed off with all this bull and takes a gun and shoots a lot of people and gets killed. He's Everyman, Peckinpah's Everyman' (quoted in Fine 2005: 275). Steven Prince suggests the ending is 'a measure of Peckinpah's displaced and implicit moralism' (1998: 193). Or is it just a measure of his self-loathing and pessimism? I'm not so sure about this notion of the film as a kind of moral tract. In the screenplay, Bennie escapes after the climactic bloodbath, carrying Al's head. But Peckinpah couldn't resist killing him off. The critic Pauline Kael, who knew the director well, discussed his fraught relationship with producers, saying 'he liked the hopelessness of it all; the role he played was the loser' (1999).

The notion of the loser is a recurring motif in Peckinpah films. In *Junior Bonner* (1972), one character asks, 'If this world is all about winners, what happens to the losers?' There is a broad streak of self-pity in Peckinpah's work as well as great compassion for the washed-up, the disillusioned and the past-it. The critic Elvis Mitchell suggests Peckinpah 'made epics about failure' while Alex Cox talks of the 'sadness that the characters have inside them' (in Weddle 1994: 367). However, this is counterbalanced to some extent by his oft-expressed interest in the work of Robert Ardrey, the screenwriter-turned-self-taught-social anthropologist, who was fashionable in the late 1960s and early 1970s (Polanski was an admirer and Stanley Kubrick often cited Ardrey when defending his *A Clockwork Orange* against charges of fascism). Ardrey argued that 'the history of man is written in blood' (quoted in Prince 1998: 105) with 'the exquisite pleasure of murder' (quoted in

Weddle 1994: 396) as our primary drive. He illustrated his arguments with evocative, if flowery, observations such as 'the propensity for violence … exists like a layer of buried molten magma underlying all human topography, seeking unceasingly some important fissure to become the most important of volcanoes' (quoted in ibid.). Indeed, Ardrey's conception of man could be applied not just to Peckinpah's work, but to the director himself:

> We were born of risen apes, not fallen angels, and the apes were armed killers besides … The miracle of man is not how far he has sunk but how magnificently he has risen. We are known among the stars for our poetry, not our corpses. (Quoted in Cagin and Dray 1994: 140).

Straw Dogs is clearly influenced by Ardrey: indeed, in 1972 Peckinpah described him as 'the only prophet alive today' (in Murray 2008: 103). But the director's cod-Darwinian pronouncements like 'everybody seems to think that man is a noble savage. But he's only an animal, a meat-eating talking animal' (quoted in Prince 1998: 106) are strikingly at odds with his empathy with and sympathy for life's losers. During his early career in theatre and television, he was a great admirer of Tennessee Williams, calling him 'easily America's greatest playwright' (quoted in Weddle 1994: 69) and stating 'I've learned more from Williams than from anyone' (ibid.) Williams' sensitivity seems at first glance an uneasy influence on 'Bloody Sam' but it's tempting to see, as David Weddle does, Peckinpah's work as offering a weird synthesis of Ardrey's savagery and Williams' compassion. The director seems to admit as much, when he says of *Alfredo Garcia*, 'it is about a love story and it is about vengeance' (in Bryson 2008: 144).

Certainly, a cursory glance at Peckinpah's public pronouncements would seem to confirm this duality. In interviews, he could be both concerned citizen ('I'm afraid to walk the streets of New York or Los Angeles' (quoted in Fine 2005: 275)) and macho boor ('Somebody asked if I hit women and I said of course I do. I believe in equal rights for women' (quoted in ibid.)), serious artist ('The truth, to me as I see it, is more important than entertainment for its own sake' (quoted in Prince 1998: v)) and chauvinist pig ('There's women and there's pussy' (quoted in Fine 2005: 275), dismissing feminists as 'those bull dykes and the crazies in their tennis sneakers and burlap sacks' (in Murray 2008: 106)). However, Mark Crispin Miller observes how, behind the bluster, many of Peckinpah's statements find echoes in his films. The director's comment on pacifism ('if a man comes up to you and cuts your hand off, you don't just offer him the other one. Not if you want to go on playing the piano you don't') can be seen as a reference to Bennie, first seen playing the piano one-handed (in Miller 1975:17). Like Hitchcock, he constructed a public persona that fed into his films, casting himself as the Holy Fool, part visionary artist, part clown and his films became a reflection of the man. Profound and lurid. Beautiful and sick. Romantic and nihilistic.

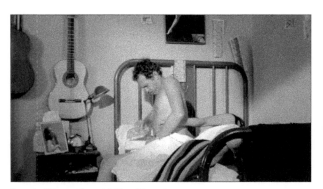

Bennie (Warren Oates) killing his crabs

The opening rural idyll

This idea of division is an important one in *Alfredo Garcia*. Birth and death, innocence and corruption, wealth and poverty. Consider how the film is awash in alcohol: the tequila Bennie and Elita slug from the bottle as they drive, toasting Alfredo. The beer he swills and spits out before ordering a bottle of brandy. The bourbon Sappensly and Quill buy him at that fateful first meeting. The tequila he uses to kill his crabs and soak Alfredo's rotting head. The whole movie has a hazy, hung-over quality (is that why Bennie always wears those shades?). In contrast, there are also frequent images of water: the film starts with a freeze-framed pond, leading into a languorous idyll for El Jefe's daughter as ducks swim by. Later, Elita and the head are both shown in the same shower. In the final scene, El Jefe's grandson, Alfredo's son, is baptised. In her Peckinpah obituary, Kathleen Murphy observes how 'Peckinpah found baptisms where he could, in tacky hotel showers, in the free flow of wine and tequila' (1984: 74). After Elita's death, Bennie washes his muddy face from a trough and the green scum coating the surface of the water indicates how far we've travelled from the opening shots of sun-splashed water.

DIGNITY AND FAILURE

There is a strong element of autobiography in all this drink and disappointment, the vengeful and the unholy. Peckinpah was from a long line of judges and the law figured prominently in his upbringing: 'My father believed in the Bible as literature, and in the law' (quoted in Weddle 1994: 42).

The world of *Alfredo Garcia* can be regarded as simultaneously exemplifying and reacting against these childhood influences: a godless world which nevertheless is steeped in religious imagery, a lawless world governed not by man-made strictures but elemental drives such as greed, lust, violence and vengeance (Murphy and Jameson consider that 'the very conceptualisation of the film is violently elemental. One has the sense of an artist loosing his personal demons in the most absolute terms he can devise' (1981: 45)). As he often does in his work, Peckinpah identifies religion with the corrupt, the ugly and the powerful. The opening images of the film, the repeated dissolves of the water, the heavily-pregnant young woman caressing her stomach and breasts, are contrasted with the interior of El Jefe's compound, this gloomy, fusty place of patriarchal power and authority, with the oil paintings and the black-clad women, the finery of El Jefe's clothes and the guards armed with rifles, the blank faces of the priests and nuns who look on impassively as this hideous old man has his daughter stripped and tortured, the gaggle of nuns who kneel before El Jefe's corpse in the final scene. Consider, too, how Bennie explains to a horrified Elita how he plans to dig up and decapitate her ex-lover:

The church cuts off the feet, fingers, any other goddamn thing from the saints, don't they? Well, what the hell? Alfredo's our saint. He's the saint of our money, and I'm gonna borrow a piece of him.

In the hotel by the cemetery, as they wait for night to fall, Elita asks Bennie if they can visit a church. 'Yeah', he answers, 'later'. They don't.

This autobiographical aspect is personified in the character of Bennie. He's a washed-up alcoholic musician working in a brothel in Mexico. Peckinpah was an alcoholic filmmaker who certainly regarded himself as washed-up, given to describing himself as a 'good whore', who spent much of his adult life in Mexico. Think of the many mirrors in Peckinpah's work, many of them shattered by bullets. 'His filmography is crowded with broken mirrors of himself' (Murphy 1984: 74). Pauline Kael suggested that the director wanted to make Oates a star but she 'didn't think he had it in him to be a star. I think Warren was imitating Sam in the picture because that was his idea of how to be a star' (in Fine 2005: 269). Kael was often a perceptive critic of Peckinpah and his work but in this instance, she's plain wrong. Oates steals *Two-Lane Blacktop* (Monte Hellman, 1971) and is very good in the same director's *Cockfighter*, playing the almost-wordless lead. It is also worth remembering that William Holden offers a career-best performance as a surrogate-Sam in *The Wild Bunch*, complete with stick-on moustache. Bennie's clothes and sunglasses, the moustache, the drink and the anger are all suggestive of Peckinpah, as is the character's progression from sweetness and charm to murderous rage. In creating a hall of mirrors, populated by various alter egos, 'conscious dopplegängers' (Kerstein 2006), Peckinpah wasn't unusual. Directors frequently use stars in such a way: think John Ford and John Wayne or Scorsese and Robert De Niro. Consider the way Hitchcock used Cary Grant as his idealised alter ego (the smooth charmer of *To Catch a Thief* (1955) or *North by Northwest* (1959)) while casting James Stewart as a darker variant (the proto-fascist intellectual in *Rope* (1948) or the romantic, broken necrophile in *Vertigo* (1958)). Similarly, Kyle MacLachlan is used as a surrogate for the boyish David Lynch of the 1980s (from *Dune* (1984) to *Twin Peaks* (1990–91)) but, by 1997, is replaced by the older Bill Pullman in *Lost Highway*. But still, the degree of identification we see in *Alfredo Garcia* is uncommon. Gordon Dawson suggests it was never supposed to be taken seriously: 'It was all camp Sam in a way', adding, 'nobody sets out to make that. I can't believe we made that movie' (in Fine 2005: 269). Consider, too, the words of Katy Haber, Peckinpah's long-suffering assistant and on/off lover, interviewed in 2007 for the BBC radio show 'I Was Sam Peckinpah's Girl Friday':

> His actors became him. William Holden was Sam in *The Wild Bunch*, Warren Oates was Sam in *Bring Me the Head of Alfredo Garcia* and Jason Robards was definitely Sam in *The Ballad of Cable Hogue*.

When Elita and Bennie enter the seedy motel near the cemetery ('a bottle of brandy and a room for the night'), she is taken aback by the squalor, the state of the room, the night manager pissing in a corner of the lobby. Bennie tells her, 'You oughta be drunk in Fresno, California. This place is a palace.' Fresno was Peckinpah's hometown. (There may be another example of this blurring between director and character in *Straw Dogs*. According to the DVD notes, Dustin Hoffman's character answers the phone and starts to give his name as David Sam (Peckinpah's first names), but given that his character is called David Sumner, this is a bit of a stretch. It is a nice idea, though.) If Peckinpah is Bennie, it is hard to avoid the impression that the powerful and sadistic El Jefe is a surrogate for James Aubrey, Head of Production at MGM who had presided over the *Pat Garrett and Billy the Kid* affair. This (very topical in the 1970s) suspicion of 'The Man' reflects Peckinpah's hatred of corporate America: he described politicians as 'killer apes right out of the caves, all dressed up in suits and talking and walking around with death in their eyes' (quoted in Seydor 1980: 269). The bounty-hunters, Sappensly and Quill, are far from the stylish hitmen of *The Killers* (Don Siegel, 1965) or *Pulp Fiction*, looking more like knackered businessmen in rumpled suits, fresh off the red eye. Like the rest of the interchangeable hoods working for El Jefe, they are loathsome for their bloodless sadism, their anonymity, their lack of humanity. Sure, Bennie is greedy, dirty, even deranged, but he is far removed from these ice-cold 'well-heeled middlemen' (Miller 1975: 8). Talking about the 'suits' in the hotel room, decadent yet icy, Mark Crispin Miller talks about how they 'demonstrate neither sexual charm nor desire' (ibid.). The women who surround them are at best ornaments, at worst irritants (such as the unfortunate whore who grabs Sappensly's crotch and gets knocked out cold). There is something sickening about these bland, colourless men: witness the revolting scene where a trouserless Max is getting a pedicure from two kneeling women and he swats one of them on the head with a magazine. Or the way they treat Bennie: referring to him scornfully as 'bartender', Max leering at him with 'you want money, don't you? Money you can spend?'

Max (Helmut Dantine) the killer ape

Presiding over this sleazy, malignant Amerika is 'Tricky Dicky' Nixon, who Peckinpah dubbed 'that cocksucker' (quoted in Seydor 1980: 269), corrupt and venal. He appears on a magazine cover in the hotel room, perfectly at home amongst whores and killers, these pampered crooks who sneer at Bennie with his clip-on tie. A caricature of the President can be glimpsed on a fake dollar bill pinned to the wall of the bar when we first meet Bennie. And Hollywood is nothing so much as another branch of Nixon's America, where scruffy drunks with big ideas are at the mercy of soulless bread-heads: the director considered it 'a whole world absolutely teeming with mediocrities, jackals, hangers-on and just plain killers' (quoted in Seydor 1980: 276).

Peckinpah is often regarded as a victim in his struggles with producers and studios, like Erich von Stroheim, Orson Welles and Nicholas Ray before him, great artists crushed by philistine moneymen. It's a familiar story, a visionary who is constrained, confounded and ultimately destroyed by the bean-counters: 'making a picture is ... I don't know ... you become in love with it ... And when you see it mutilated and cut to pieces, it's like losing a child or something' (quoted in Fine 2005: 101).

But the reality may be more complicated than that. One of the first examples of this conflict between art and money was von Stroheim's *Greed* (1925). An epic adaptation of the novel by Frank Norris, the film was originally ten hours in length but Irving Thalberg of MGM took it away from the director and had it cut down, first to four hours, then to 140 minutes. Most of the footage considered extraneous was incinerated. It's a familiar story, all too familiar to Peckinpah, as well as Welles (*The Magnificent Ambersons* (1942)), Polanski (*Dance of the Vampires* (1967)), Leone (*Once Upon a Time in America* (1984)) and countless others. But Irene Mayer, Louis B.'s daughter and the wife of Irving Thalberg, was one of the

few who saw von Stroheim's cut and she tells a different story: 'It was masterful in ways and parts of it were riveting but
it was an exhausting experience; the film in conception was a
considerable exercise in self-indulgence' (quoted in Thomson
2004b: 126). For David Thomson, exhaustion was the aim of
von Stroheim's exercise:

> Stroheim's *Greed* was not made to please, to reassure,
> to entertain or to encourage the processes of dreaming
> and fantasy. Instead it was an attempt to fling odious
> alternatives in the public's face. I believe that Stroheim
> meant to film aggressively and offensively, and for 1925,
> his way of seeing people was as important as the film's
> length … Stroheim gambled mightily with this venture;
> he must have understood the risk he was running mak-
> ing an impossible, unshowable film. (2004b:124)

Flinging odious alternatives at the viewer, filming aggressively
and offensively, an impossible, unshowable film … all charges that could be levelled at Peckinpah and *Alfredo Garcia*.
What needs to be stressed is the fact that as well as being
great artists, many of the abovementioned directors were indeed gamblers, tragic heroes with more than their share of
fatal flaws. Von Stroheim and Welles were egomaniacs, Ray
was a drunken dope-fiend and Peckinpah had a rare talent for
self-destruction. It seems a bit redundant to point this out,
given his well-documented excesses: four marriages (two to
the same woman), his violence, his decades of alcoholism
and the debilitating cocaine habit that he developed at the
comparatively late age of fifty and continued with, on and
off, after the heart attack that led to him having a pacemaker
fitted, and up to his death. In an interview the year before
Pat Garrett and Billy the Kid, the director said 'sometimes
things happen to us because we want them to' (quoted in

Weddle 1994: 483) and, like Bennie, some perverse masochistic side of Peckinpah seems to have driven him to fuck
stuff up. Pauline Kael noted:

> a tendency among some young film enthusiasts to view
> him as an icon of artistic integrity. I don't think they
> want to understand the role he played in baiting the ex-
> ecutives. He needed their hatred to stir up his own. He
> didn't want to settle fights or to compromise or even,
> maybe, to win. He wanted to draw a line and humiliate
> the executives. He simply wasn't a reasonable person.
> He made it impossible for the executives to keep their
> dignity. (1999)

In the 2004 documentary *Sam Peckinpah's West*, Thomson
describes *Alfredo Garcia* as 'a complete failure commercially', before adding, 'I suspect he [Peckinpah] was more drawn
to making complete failures than making complete successes.' Elsewhere, he considered that in Peckinpah's work 'little mattered except the self-destructive passion of the men'
(2004a: 13). This penchant for self-destruction reached its
inevitable nadir on *Convoy*, based on the novelty record (!) by
C. W. McCall. During the shoot, Peckinpah spent hours holed
up in his trailer, snorting coke. Screenwriter Rudy Wurlitzer
discovered him semi-naked with a live goat and a cocked
.38. His drug psychosis got so bad that he telephoned his
nephew, David, from the set, claiming that Steve McQueen
and the Executive Car Leasing Company were going to kill
him. Indeed, as we shall see later in this chapter, some critics
have suggested that *Alfredo Garcia* is nothing so much as a
manifestation of this self-destructiveness, a wilful attempt by
the director to drive away audiences and trash his legacy.

Admitting Peckinpah's demented masochism, however,
shouldn't absolve Aubrey. Nicknamed 'the smiling cobra' and

dismissed by James Coburn as 'a cocksucker [who] got his kicks destroying films that other people made' (in Fine 2005: 259–60), Aubrey was brought in to turn around the fortunes of an ailing MGM, crippled by a series of flops and the massive expense of building the MGM Grand Hotel in Las Vegas. *Pat Garret and Billy the Kid* was one of a number of films that fell victim to Aubrey's cost-cutting and Peckinpah's resentment and disillusion helped to fuel the black mood of *Alfredo Garcia* (according to Peckinpah associate John Bryson, the director considered having 'El Indio' Fernandez come up from Mexico to have Aubrey killed (see Fine 2005: 257–8)). This makes the end of the film, where Bennie opens fire on El Jefe and his cohorts, a kind of deathwish/suicide fantasy. He (and the director) get to strike back at all of the rich, powerful creeps on their 'shit list'. Terence Butler considers the whole film to be the director's attempt 'to confront the forces that oppress him' (1979: 9).

Certainly, Peckinpah was not shy about expressing his contempt for the studio suits who, time after time, had stepped in to slash his budgets, re-edit his work and, on *The Cincinnati Kid*, replace him with Norman Jewison. In 1972, he declared:

> This isn't a game. There's too much at stake. And the woods are full of killers, all sizes, all colours … You know, you put in your time, you pay your dues and these cats come in and destroy you … There are people all over the place, dozens of them, that I'd like to kill, quite literally kill. (Quoted in Seydor 1980: 275)

David Thomson has argued that Bennie's quest, this gory deathtrip that ends horribly, can be seen as a metaphor for filmmaking:

For Peckinpah and for Bennie, there is a sort of dignity in the job. If the world is that chaotic and that terrible and that awful, what can you cling to? Well, a job. Maybe that's why you make films. It's a job.

Similarly, Roger Ebert says in *Sam Peckinpah's West* that the film is 'a story of a man's dogged obsession to complete his task in the face of overwhelming anguish'. If one accepts this notion, that Bennie's mission is akin to Peckinpah's Sisyphean struggles in the film industry, it is useful to compare the end of the film to the climactic bloodbath in *Taxi Driver*. Unlike Scorsese, Peckinpah offers no catharsis, little release or pleasure: he even withholds any bravura cinematic technique, offering only a perfunctory, choppily-edited anti-climax. We don't see Benny die, in marked contrast to *The Wild Bunch* or *Bonnie and Clyde*, but there is no coyness masquerading as mythologising either, as in *Butch Cassidy and the Sundance Kid* (George Roy Hill, 1969) and *Thelma and Louise* (Ridley Scott, 1991). So effective is this 'anti-pleasure' ending that questions often turn up on the IMDb talk boards, viewers feeling that their copy of the film is missing footage. It is no coincidence that Fred C. Dobbs in *The Treasure of the Sierra Madre* also dies an ignominious offscreen death to similar, anti-climactic effect. No, Bennie's victory is a hollow one, so hollow it barely seems like a victory at all.

That last shot: Peckinpah's credit superimposed over the gun that kills Benny. Has anybody used their screen credit with quite the same effect? Think of William Holden's 'If they move, kill 'em' followed by the director's name in *The Wild Bunch*, or the feeding birds and exploding building that accompanies it in *The Killer Elite*. The ending of *Alfredo Garcia* is a haunting one, both anti-climactic and cruel. It also plays like a kind of squalid suicide, far from the glorious drawn-out martyrdom bestowed on *The Wild Bunch*. Kathleen Murphy

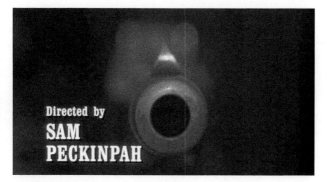

Signifying nothing

and Richard Jameson talk of 'one final hole – in the ground, in a woman, in the end of a gun' (1981: 48). It's hard to think of a last shot quite so hopeless. Except it isn't the last shot. The film does end with Bennie's death, but freeze-framed images from the film are played out under the credits. We see Bennie and Elita, Sappensly and Quill, the biker-would-be rapist. The penultimate still is an image from the opening scene, the pregnant daughter lying by the water. Just as one starts to suspect that there is a pleasing symmetry to the narrative, the last freeze-frame appears – Sappensly in his black safari suit, looking into the sack at the head within. It's a strange yet fitting last shot: a badly-dressed hired killer looking at the head, this gruesome McGuffin which we are never allowed a good look at.

NARRATIVE: LAZINESS, HAZINESS AND SLOW-MOTION

The film owes much of its unique power to its weird structure, this narrative described by David Weddle as 'tenuous' (1994: 495), full of echoes, strange contrivances, the kind of odd repetitions that occur in nightmares or drug trips. Events

are doubled up, there are digressions and coincidences, reso-
nances and blurs, reinforced by the washed-out colours and
the muddy sound.

> As in a dream, the people, objects, landscape and events
> in 'Alfredo Garcia' were constantly transmogrifying, tak-
> ing wild and improbable leaps in continuity and logic.
> (Ibid.)

This bizarre narrative approach is easily dismissed as lazy,
muddled and slipshod, but it also calls to mind Stanley
Kubrick's desire to 'explode the narrative structure' (Krohn
1992) with his *Full Metal Jacket* (1987), creating 'not only
fragmentation and aimlessness but also a mixture of styles
and modes' (Naremore 2007: 211). The narrative itself seems
to be as drunk as Bennie: meandering, talky stretches punctu-
ated by bursts of violence, woozy and staggering. For Steven
Prince, Bennie is also the key, being 'not just the emblem of
death but the destroyer of narrative' (1998: 192). Are we supposed to think that this whole thing is playing out in Bennie's
head?

Plot elements, *mise-en-scène* and dialogue all combine to
create layers of meaning, hazy and half-understood. Our first
glimpse of Alfredo is in the locket that contains a photo of
his head. Bennie teases Elita about her affair with Alfredo,
asking her 'did he give you good head?' In reply, she tells
him 'don't play with my head'. Often the framing cuts the
heads off characters. Events double up, repeat, echo. The
biker tears Elita's shirt off, mirroring the opening scenes
where El Jefe's daughter is stripped to the waist. Buses appear on two occasions, one nearly crashing into Bennie and
Elita, one turning up as the Garcia family come to collect the
head. There are two tyre blow-outs that play a significant role
in the narrative. The first leads to Elita and Bennie camping

out, the near-rape and the film's first murders; the second slows up the bounty-hunters, enabling Bennie to catch them up. Bennie accuses Elita of pretending to be sick with a cold when she was cuckolding him with Alfredo; when the bikers arrive, one of them says something about catching a cold from a woman, Kristofferson's biker blowing his nose when he sits by the fire. Elita and Alfredo are doubled, as she goes from the hotel shower to Alfredo's grave while the head is unearthed and ends up under the same shower. But the best example of this mirroring occurs with Bennie and Alfredo. The latter was killed driving home from his tryst with Elita and Bennie nearly crashes the car as he kisses her while driving. Quill mentions that Garcia spoke Spanish, English and a little French while Bennie refers to money as 'pain, bread, dinero'. By the end of the film, Bennie and Alfredo have become one: 'Just tell them Alfredo Garcia is here', he tells the guards at El Jefe's place. As if to emphasise the negativity on show here, the film is book-ended by echoed cries of 'No!'. El Jefe's wife cries out as her daughter is tortured, Bennie screams it repeatedly as he kills the bodyguards in the compound and says it again quietly, before shaking his head and shooting El Jefe. When Sappensly asks Bennie if he knows Alfredo, there is the sound of a car crash and it is unclear whether it is a diegetic sound from the street outside or just in Bennie's head, a premonition or a way of doubling both men in death (Bennie, too, will die in his car). These contrivances and echoes help to create a narrative which is both 'self-conscious and bleakly playful' (Prince 1998: 208). There is also, possibly, another allusion to Huston's *The Treasure of the Sierra Madre* in the way that Bennie seems to be at the mercy of malign forces, forces described by the grizzled Howard as 'a great joke played on us by the Lord or fate or nature'. Note how in both films, bad fortune comes to the protagonists disguised as luck. In Huston's film, penniless losers Dobbs and Curtin

(Tim Holt) happen to walk into the flophouse just in time to hear Howard's stories about prospecting gold. Later, as the men pool their cash only to discover they are 600 bucks short, up pops the street kid who pestered Dobbs into buying a lottery ticket, telling him he's won 200 pesos. Without these strokes of what seems like luck, their ill-fated trip would not have happened, the gold would still be in the mountain and Dobbs would be alive. In much the same way, a series of chance meetings (Sappensly and Quill's initial questioning of Bennie, their later appearance as the Garcia family take back the head) and accidents (the burst tyre, the arrival of the bus that enables Bennie to get his gun) that seem to be fortuitous only end up leading Elita and Bennie to the grave.

The dialogue seems emblematic of this 'strange complexity', often hard-boiled and pulpy to the point of being camp, yet delivered by the cast as if they really mean it: take Quill's 'if your information is wrong, you too are wrong. Dead wrong.' Or how about El Jefe's plaintive 'he was like a son to me'? Bennie gets all the best lines, however: snarling at the bikers, 'you guys are definitely on my shit list'; to Elita, after shooting his gun at a flock of birds, 'Hell, I wasn't trying to hit 'em, you know?'; ordering a drink with 'a double bourbon with a champagne back, none of your tijano bullshit, and fuck off'; his heart-rending 'I love you' as he sits under the shower with Elita; addressing onlookers with the surreal 'don't look at me with your goddamn fuckin' eyes'. The last quote is an important one, I think. This is a film about looking. Consider Bennie's shades, worn in bed but not on a bright sunny day, the way he flinches when he's photographed with them off or the fact that he can barely look at his reflection without them. And there are the mirrors we see in at least five scenes. But it is also a film about what we don't see, this being, paradoxically, both Peckinpah's most violent film and one of his most restrained. We don't get a good look at the severed head, we

A weirdly discreet horror

don't see Alfredo's corpse or Elita or Bennie die. The best illustration of this paradox is the scene where Bennie shoots one of the wounded bounty-hunters lying on the ground. The shot flips the man over onto his back and Bennie asks himself 'Why? Because it feels so damned good', before shooting him again. This scene, described by Steven Prince as 'perverse and horrible, but lyrically so' (1998: 195) would seem, given the director's 'Bloody Sam' image, to be overkill to the point of self-parody: Murphy and Jameson suggest as much, saying of the shooting and its aftermath, with Bennie throwing the head into the car (and at the camera), 'it's as though the director were saying "This is what you think I am: this is what you came for. Well, here it is!"' (1981: 48). But the self-conscious framing of the shot means our view of the man lying on the floor is hidden by an open car door and the last shot (fired into his head?) goes unseen. The final frame of the film, Sappensly gazing at a sight we never see, the head in a sack, is another illustration of this weirdly discreet horror. The framing of shots throughout the film is often strange, suggesting contrived artlessness or carelessness, it's hard to say which. It could be both. Some scenes are characterised

The cluttered frame

by the kind of seeming impatience with form that occurs often in many Fassbinder films or Woody Allen's work from the
early 1990s (*Husbands and Wives* (1992), *Manhattan Murder
Mystery* (1993)), while the choppy editing often feels like a
lesser director ripping off the Peckinpah style: indeed, the
weird cutting of the shoot-out in El Jefe's compound resembles nothing so much as Michael Winner's films (such as the
painful *Dirty Weekend* (1993)). It is certainly very far from the
accomplished use of form displayed in the director's previous
films and although he would go on to make some bad films,
there would be nothing quite so strikingly odd. Even inciden-
tal scenes are framed in such a bizarre fashion as to be disorientating: when Bennie enters the Hotel Camino Real, we
see him reflected in a wall-mounted mirror as he approaches
the desk. The *mise-en-scène* is often excessive, the frame
cluttered with garish décor, crowded with people. Often this
approach is used to great effect, creating a sense of disor-
der and mess: look how cramped Bennie's room feels, the
stuff on the walls, Elita's guitar, her rolling out of bed and
tumbling to the floor. Or when Bennie stands there in the
half-light, a cigarette hanging out of his mouth, unsheathing

the machine: behind him the frame is full with the bed, the open wardrobe, the postcards and photos, the lamp with the dangling cord. Or the scene in the bar where Bennie works, the master shots stuffed with bodies, Bennie, Sappensly and Quill, the whores and the punters. This clutter that seems to make up Bennie's world is contrasted with the airy anonymity of the hotel rooms where El Jefe's hoods hang out, the space, the wooden doors set in this great wooden wall, the pastel colours. If, as the Italian horror auteur Dario Argento has suggested, 'buildings are like your inside ... buildings are

Buildings are like souls

souls' (quoted in Reesman 2008: 71–2) we can regard Bennie as a mess and the sleazy hotel-dwellers as a bunch of anonymous blanks.

Particularly noteworthy is the cavalier use of slow-motion, the formal device most associated with the director: as the veteran Howard Hawks wryly noted, 'I can kill ten guys in the time it takes him to kill one' (quoted in Fine 2005: 151). Peckinpah wasn't the first director to utilise slow-motion in his action scenes: Henri-Georges Clouzot in *Le salaire de la peur* (*The Wages of Fear*,1953), Akira Kurosawa in *Shichinin no samurai* (*The Seven Samurai*, 1954) and Arthur Penn in *The Left-Handed Gun* (1958) and, most notably, *Bonnie and Clyde*. But the fact that Peckinpah became synonymous with slow-motion action scenes is a testament to how he mastered the technique. As well as the aforementioned Monty Python sketch 'Sam Peckinpah's Salad Days' (see introduction), the director's use of slow-motion was also parodied in a sketch from *The Benny Hill Show*. Add to that John Belushi's Peckinpah skit from an episode of *Saturday Night Live* where his working method involves brutalising an actress, and it is clear just how much of a 'cult of personality' surrounded 'Bloody Sam' and just how strongly he was identified with stylistically excessive violence. Who out of today's crop of directors could be so accurately skewered in popular entertainment shows?[2]

Peckinpah set out to avoid the use of whole slow-motion scenes and instead would interweave footage filmed by six cameras filming at various speeds, creating an effect that was simultaneously exhilarating, sickening and disorientating. According to the director, his desire to use slow-motion arose from witnessing an act of violence whilst on military service in China. However, he couldn't get his story straight, telling one interviewer how he was on a train when 'a bullet tore through a window and into a nearby Chinese passenger,

Slow-motion and the messy business of death

killing him immediately … I noticed that time slowed down'
(quoted in Weddle 1994: 55). Yet elsewhere, he claimed he
was the victim: 'I was shot and I remember falling down and
it was so long' (quoted in Fine 2005: 24). Wherever his in-
spiration came from, after a faltering start with the botched
Major Dundee, he mastered the technique, with *The Wild
Bunch* shocking and thrilling audiences in equal measure with
violence both graphic and graceful. As David Weddle puts it,
'the action would constantly be shifting from slow to fast to
slower still to fast again, giving time within the sequences a
strange elastic quality' (1994: 334). In *Straw Dogs*, he modi-
fied his style further, integrating slow-motion flash inserts
into scenes. But in *Alfredo Garcia*, the technique seems to
be applied in an almost random fashion, such as the slowed-
down scene of a bus careering though mud (!). There are
repeated shots of bodies falling to the ground, limbs askew
and hair flopping, emphasising the ugly mechanics of death.
Here, the slow-motion footage smacks of a kind of authorial self-loathing, a cavalier, even pedestrian use of his stylistic trademark. There are some striking moments, however,
when Peckinpah uses it as effectively as he ever did, such as
the shot when Bennie, lying in the grave, lets go of Elita and
she slips out of his embrace and back into the soil.

GENRE

Generically, *Alfredo Garcia* is, on the surface, a kind of love
story-cum-horror film. But there are more genres and cycles
thrown into the mix, including the then-voguish road movie,
the western and the buddy movie. The road has traditionally represented opportunity and escape in American culture,
the notion of the quest an important one that taps into the
pioneer spirit. In literature (*The Adventures of Huckleberry
Finn* (1884) by Mark Twain, *As I Lay Dying* (1930) by William

Faulkner, *The Grapes of Wrath* (1939) by John Steinbeck) and film (*It Happened One Night* (Frank Capra, 1934), *You Only Live Once* (Fritz Lang, 1937), *The Wizard of Oz* (Victor Fleming, 1939)), the idea of Americans as a rootless people engaged in the search for a place to call home is a recurring one (and one that continues beyond the stars in Spielberg's *E. T. The Extra-Terrestrial* (1982)). There was a dark side of the road, however, which is best portrayed in *Detour* (1945), Edgar Ulmer's nightmare uber-noir shot in five days. The 1960s and the notion of 'dropping out' saw the road movie re-emerge, a perfect vehicle (pardon the pun) for the 'passive hero' imported from the European art movie, a stoned rebel without a cause. *Easy Rider* (Dennis Hopper, 1969), *Two-Lane Blacktop*, *Five Easy Pieces* (Bob Rafelson, 1970), *Vanishing Point* (Richard C. Sarafian, 1971) and a host of lesser films saw the road as offering an alternative to 'straight society', albeit one that often ended unhappily: *Easy Rider*, *Vanishing Point* and *Dirty Mary, Crazy Larry* (John Hough, 1974) all end in death while the rootless protagonist of *Five Easy Pieces* just keeps moving on. The most striking finale is that offered in *Two-Lane Blacktop* where, stealing an idea from Ingmar Bergman's *Persona* (1966), the car literally burns up the screen. In *Alfredo Garcia*, when we first meet Bennie, he is a passive drifter, declaring that 'I've been no place I want to go back to, that's for damn sure'. This may be yet another echo of *The Treasure of the Sierra Madre*, where another misplaced gringo, Curtin, says bitterly 'all places are the same to me'. But Peckinpah's view of the road is the bleakest since Ulmer's: Bennie may as well be driving round and round in circles, knocking back tequila from the bottle. As he comes undone, so too does his car, the gleaming red convertible he sets off in becoming a grimy wreck, the bodywork battered and the windscreen caked in dust. The endless possibilities offered by the open road come down to this: Bennie, muddied and bloodied, waving the flies away and opening the window to rid himself of the stink of rotting flesh. As one reviewer commented '*Everything* in the world that this movie depicts is inescapably tainted, grubby, and dirty' (Jon 2007; emphasis in original). *Alfredo Garcia* seems to have marked a turning point for the sub-genre: the year after Peckinpah's film, Oates took another ill-fated road trip (with Peter 'Captain America' Fonda) in *Race with the Devil* (Jack Starrett, 1975), only to be hunted by backwoods satanists, and these ill-starred journeys became the template for later road movies such as *Something Wild* (Jonathan Demme, 1986), *Natural Born Killers* (Oliver Stone, 1994) and *The Doom Generation* (Gregg Araki, 1995). In their introduction to *The Road Movie Book*, Steven Cohan and Ina Rae Hark identify a group of films within the road movie sub-genre, concerned with outlaw couples. Although not a new phenomenon (with examples going back as far as the above-mentioned Fritz Lang film and Nicholas Ray's debut *They Live By Night* (1948)) Cohan and Hark argue that this is a cycle that really came into its own in the 1970s, with 'the deferral of sexual intimacy' seen in classical Hollywood films no longer plausible for audiences and consequently 'heterosexual road movies had to derive their frisson instead from implicating the couple's sexual union in a wider tapestry of violence which became just another version of their relationship' (1997: 9). Peckinpah's film fits this template, with its mix of heartfelt romance and brutal violence, a mixture that would be pushed to absurd extremes in the Southern Gothic of David Lynch's *Wild at Heart* (1990).

The opening minutes of the film suggest a western. The men who come to collect El Jefe's daughter are wearing sombreros and jangling spurs, there's a rider on horseback and abundant cacti. There is nothing in El Jefe's mansion to indicate it is the 1970s. So it comes as jarring to the viewer when we see aeroplanes and screeching cars (Peckinpah used a camel to similar disorientating effect in the opening of *Ride the High Country*). The western is also the American genre most strongly associated with Mexico. Although it has had a home-grown film industry since the early twentieth century, the country has been ill-served by Hollywood, portrayed as a lawless place of sleaze and death (the kind of place evoked in the song 'Hey Joe', where the eponymous character shoots 'his woman down', before 'heading down to Mexico way, where a man can be free'). Outside of the western and the travelogue images of froth like the Elvis Presley picture *Fun in Acapulco* (Richard Thorpe, 1963) and *The Real Cancun* (Rick de Oliviera, 2003), Hollywood's Mexico takes in the seedy motels and knife-wielding hoods of *Touch of Evil* (Orson Welles, 1958), the brothels and rapes of *Revenge* (Tony Scott, 1990), the sickly yellows of the drug drama *Traffic* (Steven Soderbergh, 2000), the corruption and kidnapping of *Man on Fire* (Tony Scott, 2004) and the cruising cowboys of *Brokeback Mountain* (Ang Lee, 2005). Like Peckinpah, John Huston lived on and off in Mexico and offered some heated, lurid visions of life south of the border: the aforementioned *The Treasure of the Sierra Madre*, Richard Burton's drunken defrocked priest in *Night of the Iguana* (1964), Albert Finney's smashed writer in *Under the Volcano* (1984), a film Peckinpah had lobbied to make. For both directors, the country offered a kind of refuge from a puritanical America. David Weddle calls Peckinpah's Mexico 'an Old Testament realm offering polarised visions of Eden and Sodom' (1994: 37). To Kathleen Murphy and Richard Jameson, it offers 'a womb-tomb where sex and death, fecundity and decomposition are not discrete but simultaneous processes' (1981: 45). According to John Kraniauskas, the film 'creates an ambiguous and mythic space out of Mexican materials, a border zone between the Mexico it so strongly refers to and the West it is not' (1993: 33). But Richard Combs, one of the few reviewers to admire the film on its initial release, points out the 'Conradian horror that overtakes Peckinpah whenever he steps outside America' (1985: 397). If one rules out *Major Dundee*, *The Wild Bunch* and *Pat Garrett and Billy the Kid* (all set largely in Mexico but also containing sequences set north of the border), the director's three films set outside the US, *Cross of Iron*, *Straw Dogs* and *Alfredo Garcia*, are his most savage (and while a film set on the Russian front in 1943 is bound to contain many violent scenes, *Straw Dogs* plays out its rape and bloodshed against the backdrop of a sleepy Cornish village). Peckinpah said of the country, 'Mexico has always meant something special to me. My Mexican experience is never over' (quoted in Thomson 2009: 34).

Of course, as a western, Peckinpah's film is far from the classic genre films of Hawks and Ford: 'in fact this revisionist western is so revisionist that it has jets, convertibles, accountants and modern Mexico City in it' (Moody 2009). Although Philip French detects elements of Ford's *The Searchers* (1956) in *Alfredo Garcia*, describing it as a 'Peckinpah favourite' (2009), the director had dismissed it as 'one of [Ford's] worst films' (in Macklin 2008: 154). But the genre had undergone considerable changes in the 1960s and 1970s, with the graphic, stylised violence of the Italian westerns and the addition of counterculture values and a great deal of moral ambiguity. Examples of such revisionist fare include the aforementioned work of Arthur Penn, the bitter Vietnam allegory *Ulzana's Raid* (Robert Aldrich, 1972), Altman's typically genre-bending *McCabe and Mrs. Miller* (1971) and the wild west ghost story *High Plains Drifter* (Clint Eastwood, 1973). *The Life and Times of Judge Roy Bean* (John Huston, 1973) was an episodic comedy western with Ava Gardner's Lillie Langtry, Stacy Keach's albino gunman and a pet bear while *Dirty Little Billy* (Stan Dragoti, 1972) starred Michael J. Pollard as a gargoylesque Billy the Kid (with the provocative tag-line 'Billy the Kid was a punk'). There were also the more self-consciously *outré* arty westerns such as Andy Warhol's playful *Lonesome Cowboys* (1968), the trippy bloodbath *El Topo* (Alejandro Jodorowsky, 1970) and the anarchic *The Last Movie*. Discussing Peckinpah's earlier work, Paul Schrader suggested, in *Sam Peckinpah's West*, that his 'contribution to the genre was like Orson Welles's contribution to the film noir … which is that he chiselled the gravestone'; but if the truth be told, the graveyard was pretty crowded with film-makers wanting to bury this most traditional of American genres. Peckinpah may have been the most accomplished of them, but what Alex Cox calls the western's 'revolution-ary tendency … postmodern, respecting neither genre nor linear narrative: the cowboy version of punk' (2006), would continue at least until the stunning *Heaven's Gate*.

With its bleakness and gore, creepy country graveyard and decapitation, *Alfredo Garcia* often resembles a gothic horror. It is possible to read the whole thing as a weird variant on the zombie film. Comparing Peckinpah to Howard Hawks, Kathleen Murphy says, 'in their darkest films, it's as though everyone is dead already' (1984: 74). To Steven Prince, Bennie is 'the walking dead' (1998: 192). It is significant that as Bennie literally rises from the grave after the seconds of black screen that follow the spade blow to his head, we get a brief point-of-view shot of his hand clawing at the soil. This raises the possibility that from that point on, we are watching the vengeful dream of a dead man. Consider, too, the use of 'Bennie's Song', sung by Elita as they drive to the cemetery. According to John Kraniauskas, the song is a Mexican popu-lar ballad called a *corrido* that 'tells us that Bennie will die … because traditionally corridos are sung to remember the dead' (1993: 33). For Phil Nugent, 'it's when Bennie emerg-es from the grave that *Alfredo Garcia* kicks into high gear' (2005). The action scenes are more stylish, the scenery – 'as if replenished by fresh blood' – is more beautiful and Oates comes into his own:

> As a would-be movie star he's an unobtrusive presence in search of a part but as a walking dead man he's scarily potent and convincingly dangerous. (Ibid.)

Bennie is a walking corpse, whose desire for revenge forces him to leave his love sharing a grave with the man who cuckolded him. This nightmare quality is reminiscent of other films that play out like death dreams: *Vertigo* where James Stewart's Scotty is left hanging from a roof at the start of the film with no way down or *Point Blank* (John Boorman, 1968), where we are never really sure if Lee Marvin's Walker is dead from the start, the events of the film just the revenge fantasy of a dying man. But a palpable sense of the gothic and the nightmarish was always there in Peckinpah's work. He worked as a writer on the paranoid classic *Invasion of the Bodysnatchers* (Don Siegel, 1956), and his first film, *The Deadly Companions*, transplanted William Faulkner to the wild west, with a decomposing corpse transported cross-country. The rural nastiness of *Straw Dogs* is evoked in horror films such as *The Wicker Man*, *An American Werewolf in London* (John Landis, 1980) and *Eden Lake* (James Watkins, 2008).

Alfredo Garcia also seems to be influenced by the buddy movie. This was a cycle of films about male duos that flourished in the New Hollywood. Whether the subjects were stoned long-hairs (as in *Easy Rider* and *Two-Lane Blacktop*) or cops (as in *Hickey and Boggs* (Robert Culp, 1972), *Freebie and the Bean* (Richard Rush, 1974) or *Busting* (Peter Hyams, 1974)), cowboys (*Butch Cassidy and the Sundance Kid*) or hipster medics (*MASH* (Robert Altman, 1968)), buddy movies celebrated male friendship and, for the most part, excluded female characters. As Bennie and Alfredo drink, drive and

shack up in motels together, Peckinpah appears to be offering up a grim satire of the cycle. Note the way that, in
time-honoured fashion, their initial antagonism changes to
something like understanding, as Bennie tells the head, 'Hell,
it wasn't your fault. I know that. But we're going to find out.
You and me.' This strange duo, the demented loser and the
decomposing head, the oddest couple of all. Perhaps inevi-
tably with all this testosterone, there was a strong streak of
homoeroticism running through the buddy movie and in an
attempt to counter this (and 'reassure' viewers as to the protagonists' 'uncomplicated' maleness), a series of lame gay
stereotypes recur throughout this cycle. After all, how can
anyone see anything sexual in Harvey Keitel and Robert De
Niro sharing a bed in *Mean Streets* (Martin Scorsese, 1973)
after we've been presented with Ken Sinclair's Sammy ('hey
fellas, you going my way?'), camping it up in his yellow mac
and white flares? After Harry Dean Stanton's appearance
as a hitchhiker who hits on Warren Oates ('I just thought it
might help you relax while you drive') in *Two Lane Blacktop*,
who could suspect anything more than camaraderie between
moody Dennis Wilson and the even-moodier James Taylor?
Even gay directors can be guilty of this, with John Schlesinger
attempting to offset the romance between Jon Voight and
Dustin Hoffman in *Midnight Cowboy* (1968) with squirming,
nerdy Bob Balaban. Robin Wood has described this device
as 'a disclaimer' (1986: 229), although sometimes, a buddy
movie will foregound this homoeroticism: in *Thunderbolt
and Lightfoot* (Michael Cimino, 1974), Clint Eastwood bonds
with a fetchingly dragged-up Jeff Bridges. With the characters of Sappensly and Quill, this woman-bashing gay partner-
ship, Peckinpah may well be mocking this bizarre tendency.
Whereas the buddy movie was perceived by some to be a
response to feminism and the perceived threat it posed to all
things masculine, Wood takes a more positive view, seeing

the cycle as offering a kind of liberation: 'If women can be dispensed with so easily, a great deal else goes with them … marriage, family, home' (1986: 227). In this light, we can see just how hopeless a vision Peckinpah offers, subverting both the road movie and the buddy movie, substituting violence and pain for the joys of the open road and homosocial camaraderie.[3]

For some, the 'masculinist' tendencies at play in the buddy movie are also evident in the cult film audience. For Mark Jancovich *et al.*:

> The aesthetics of transgression that underpins so much cult movie fandom is often directly opposed to the values of domesticity that are not only associated with femininity but for which women have historically been presumed to [have] been responsible. (2003: 3)

Significantly, all of the genres/cycles that can be discerned in the mishmash of Peckinpah's film flourished in the late 1960s and early 1970s, in part due to the perceived anti-establishment credentials of films from the period as varied as *Night of The Living Dead, Five Easy Pieces, Little Big Man* and *MASH*. Weirdly, Peckinpah was embraced by the counterculture of the period. This was, in no small part, due to his casting of musicians such as Kristofferson and Bob Dylan (who scored and appeared in *Pat Garrett and Billy the Kid*). But there was also his carefully-contrived outlaw persona, the beard and bandana, the drink and drugs. In interviews, he spoke out against Nixon and the war in Vietnam. The controversy surrounding *The Wild Bunch* also played a part, particularly the suggestion that its opening scenes (with vicious Americans in uniform slaughtering civilians) referenced the war.

There is an admitted irony in the fact that 'The Love Generation' flocked to see such violent cinematic fare, from

Bonnie and Clyde to *A Clockwork Orange*, particularly when a number of these films seem to consciously bait their hippy audiences: consider Popeye Doyle (Gene Hackman) in *The French Connection* (William Friedkin, 1971) and his credo of 'never trust a nigger … never trust anyone', or the rapist/murderer of *Dirty Harry* (Don Siegel, 1971) with his long hair and peace-sign belt-buckle. But all the anger and acid of the late 1960s meant that psychosis was never faraway, both onscreen and off: the Weathermen, the Manson Murders and the way über-hippy Dennis Hopper morphed into the villainous perverts of *Out of the Blue* (Dennis Hopper, 1983) and *Blue Velvet* (David Lynch, 1986). This sense of disillusion, the harsh comedown after the heady trip of the 'Summer of Love', feeds into many 1970s films and *Alfredo Garcia* is no exception. (In truth, Peckinpah was, in the vernacular of the time, a bit of a square. He didn't know who Dylan was when the singer expressed an interest in working with him and when they did meet, the director tried to impress Dylan by telling him he was a big Roger Miller fan.) Although he was no hippy, he was deeply affected by the war in Vietnam and this fed his loathing for Nixon. As an ex-serviceman, he was particularly outraged and saddened by the slaughter of civilians in the village of My Lai in 1969, even going so far as to write a letter to Lieutenant William Calley, the man convicted over his role in the massacre. Vietnam, like the Nixon presidency, seems to bleed into many of Peckinpah's films, in much the same way that the Holocaust bleeds into the noirs of the 1940s or the atrocities in Iraq, from Internet beheadings to the torture photos from Abu Ghraib prison, have made their mark on contemporary horror films like *Saw* (James Wan, 2004), *Wolf Creek* (Greg McLean, 2006) and *Hostel* (Eli Roth, 2006). Peckinpah seems to have been aware of the topicality of the film. In a letter to the Swedish Censorship Board, responding to their decision to ban *Alfredo Garcia*, he acknowledged that 'some people may find my films difficult and even terrifying but they cannot ignore the world today' (quoted in Prince 1998: 228). In interviews, Peckinpah offered a pessimistic, despairing view of 1970s America: 'You know what this country's all about, doctor? It's brainwashing, it's bullshit. It's hustling products and people, making no distinctions between the two. We're in the Dark Ages again' (in Murray 2008: 118). His cure for this bleak situation? 'We have to water the flowers – and screw a lot' (2008: 119). Like a great many social critics, Peckinpah is better on diagnosing the problem than offering a solution: it isn't for nothing that he told interviewer Barbara Walters 'that it was not in his power to present constructive values in his work' (quoted in Prince 1998: 145).

WOMEN

Then there is the question of women. With the possible exception of slow-motion violence, nothing says Peckinpah like misogyny, accusations of it swarming round his work like the flies around Alfredo's head. The chief area of debate concerns the director's depiction of sexual violence, where the line separating seduction from coerced sex/rape is frequently blurred, if not dissolved completely. The most notorious example of this is *Straw Dogs*, where Peckinpah's avowed intention to 'shoot the best rape scene that's ever been shot' (Thomson 2002a) led to the film being unavailable for home viewing in the UK from 1984 to 2002. There are thematically similar incidents in *The Getaway* and *Cross of Iron* (indeed, one might argue that any filmmaker who stages even one rape/seduction is skating on pretty thin ice). Unlike some critics, I do not intend to tie myself in knots defending Peckinpah on this score: his attitude to his female characters is frequently unpleasant and often troubling. Gabrielle Murray

is almost euphemistic when she talks of his 'sometimes ab-
berant treatment of the representation of women' (2002). It
is, however, undeniable that some of the most perceptive
commentators on his oeuvre tend to be female, including
Murray, Pauline Kael and Kathleen Murphy. The character of
Elita is one of the more complex of Peckinpah's women but
this might not be saying much. She is frequently undressed
(and was the subject of a *Playboy* spread shot on the set) but
given Peckinpah's oft-quoted claim to be 'like a whore ... I go
where I'm kicked' (in Bryson 2008: 143), it is possible to see
her as another of the director's surrogates. Indeed, for Mark
Crispin Miller, all of the characters are selling themselves: he
dubs Bennie 'a whore lost in a world of whores' (1975: 9).
The director suggested that the women in *Alfredo Garcia* are
the 'positive poles ... the lifeforce and instinct' (quoted in
Prince 1998: 149), and if this is the case, it speaks volumes
about the world of the film that they are stripped, abducted,
abused and killed. Steven Prince relates the experience of
Garner Simmons, author of *Peckinpah: A Portrait in Montage*
(1982) and a friend of the director, who was there for the
Alfredo Garcia shoot, and who recalled how, as Peckinpah
filmed El Jefe's hoods breaking his daughter's arm, the director's 'eyes filled with tears' (1998: 160). Prince regards
this 'grieving response' as 'an indice of humane perspective'
(ibid.) but I am not so sure. Peckinpah reportedly cried easily, bursting into tears at Dylan's songs for *Pat Garrett and
Billy the Kid* and while filming the climactic battle in *Cross of
Iron*. It is also worth remembering D. H. Lawrence's dictum,
often quoted by Robin Wood, that one should 'never trust the
artist – trust the tale' (Wood 1999: 171), and by that measure, Peckinpah's treatment of his women (onscreen and off)
is disturbing. The scene where the two bikers (played by
Donnie Fritts and a hirsute Kris Kristofferson) happen upon
Bennie and Elita is creepily opaque. While one of the men

'I've been here before and you don't know the way'

holds Bennie at gunpoint, Elita tries to reassure him as the other man drags her away, saying, 'I've been here before and you don't know the way.' Out of sight of the others, her abductor uses his flick knife to slit her shirt before tearing it off, the framing of the shot revealing the yin and yang patch and the cross on his denim jacket. The score here is intrusive, creepy and discordant (the film's soundtrack album labels this piece 'Prelude to a Rape'). Elita slaps the biker twice before he slaps her back, only to reach out to caress her gently. Then he stops and walks away, lost in some sort of existential biker fug, sitting down and picking at a blade of grass. Back at the campfire, we can sense a weird kind of camaraderie between Bennie and his captor. When Bennie snarls, 'What the hell, she can handle it a lot better than I can', the biker replies, 'she sure can'. Even under these circumstances, men bond with each other more easily than they do with the women they love. The biker plays Elita's guitar as he sings to the increasingly pissed-off Bennie, who sits glowering by the light of the fire. The song he sings, 'Bad Blood Baby', was written by Peckinpah and the salacious lyrics seem to be mocking Bennie and his predicament:

Ain't it driving you insane?/Well, he's eaten up all your candy/ain't it turning [sic] up your brain?/She's got bad blood baby/ ... Well he's got her on her back now, showing him just what she's got'.

Elita's mood appears to change and, still topless, she follows the biker and kneels before him. There is a blank expression on Vega's face which manages to be simultaneously erotic and eerie as she whispers, 'Please don't', then after a meaningful pause, 'please'. They kiss passionately and it is clear that she is a willing participant. They move until she is, in the words of the song, 'lying on her back now' with the biker above her, and it is this sight that greets Bennie when he arrives, gun in hand. Peckinpah was fascinated by questions of loyalty and betrayal: it is a recurring theme in his work and this sequence is a good example of this. Indeed, it was one of the first scenes the writers came up with. As mentioned earlier, Frank Kowalski was interested in writing about Caryl Chessman, the 'Red Light Bandit'. Unlike the many artists (including Ray Bradbury, Lenny Bruce and Aldous Huxley) who regarded Chessman as the victim of a miscarriage of justice, Kowalski was more interested in his crimes: 'He used to rape girls and then take off. That idea intrigued me and Sam: what if someone was raping your girl and you had to stand and watch?' (in Fine 2005: 267). This scenario, with its associations of impotence and rage, violence and betrayal, seems to be one Peckinpah tormented himself with and it recurs in his work: he doesn't identify with the raped Amy (Susan George) in *Straw Dogs* but rather with her unsuspecting husband, David (Dustin Hoffman), lured away on a phony duck hunt. He doesn't side with the abducted, raped Sally Struthers in *The Getaway* but rather with her humiliated husband, who is tied to a chair and forced to watch as she cavorts (willingly? Semi-willingly?) with her abductor. The Kristofferson character goes from a leering, grinning creep with a gun at the campfire to a soulful, almost dreamy charmer once he is alone with Elita and she responds in a way that illustrates Bennie's (and, seemingly, the director's) worst fears. His female characters are slapped, shot, raped, drugged and strangled: David Thomson's (slightly breathless?) observation that 'in Peckinpah films, women must expect to get stripped to their white brave breasts. It comes with the territory, like being smashed in the face' (2009: 35) actually seems to downplay the worst of these excesses (the aforementioned Amy or the naked woman (Merete Van Kamp) in the opening minutes of *The Osterman Weekend*, whose post-coital masturbating is interrupted by assassins who kill her with an injection to the face). Still, Peckinpah seems to rarely, if ever, empathise with these suffering women, just with the men who love them. Not with Elita, led off, stripped and slapped but with Bennie, sat by the campfire, making threats and drinking tequila.

She, like many Peckinpah women, is 'collateral damage' (Kerstein 2006) in this struggle between men. The fact that she reacts so passionately to her would-be rapist rubs further salt into Bennie's wounds: we don't know why she kisses the biker but we do know how Bennie feels when he sees her doing it. It's about the men, the losers, the suckers, the cuckolded and the humiliated. This ambiguity and cruelty we sense in Peckinpah's depictions of women are important, adding a dark dimension which can make the viewer uncomfortable (indeed, the unsimulated cruelty to animals in some of the director's films – the decapitated chickens, exploding lizards, tripped horses and burning arachnids – seems to perform a similar function). A big part of this discomfort is the lack of a clear context for all this sexual violence, the authorial point of view often unclear. In Martin Barker's characteristically thoughtful piece on audience reactions to *Straw Dogs*, 'Loving and Hating *Straw Dogs*: The Meanings of Audience Responses to a Controversial Film' (2006), he refers to an article written by Charles Barr for *Screen* in 1972. Barr examined the tendency among many critics to defend Kubrick's *A Clockwork Orange* while condemning Peckinpah (for example, the 13 British critics who wrote to the *Times*, describing *Straw Dogs* as 'dubious in its intention, excessive in its effect' (Barr 1972: 17)). As Barker puts it:

> Barr makes a still-compelling case that those who hated Peckinpah's film so much were expressing a fear of 'contamination' – because the film did not permit distancing from the ambiguities of feeling which the actions and events of the film portrayed. (2006)

This fear of 'contamination' may explain a lot of the revulsion towards Peckinpah's treatment of sexual violence, which is so often 'a strange mix of the explicit and the oblique' (Kermode 2003).

Is Elita offering herself up to protect Bennie? Is she turned on by the situation? Does it matter? It is part of the power of Peckinpah's work, this ability to unnerve and provoke, to scratch at something until it starts to bleed. Writer/director

Paul Schrader has talked of how Peckinpah's work inspired him 'to go into your neuroses, to go into those things about yourself that you fear, not to cover them up but to open them up' (in Weddle 1994: 12). It is also, surely, a bit of a dead-end to judge films largely on their espousal of 'progressive' values. One may get a warm, fuzzy feeling from the liberal platitudes of *Cry Freedom* (Richard Attenborough, 1987) or *Philadelphia* (Jonathan Demme, 1993) but would anybody try to argue seriously that they are better films than unpleasant, even depressing works such as *The Birth of a Nation* (D. W. Griffith, 1915), *Triumph des Willens* (*Triumph of the Will*, Leni Riefenstahl, 1935) or *Mandingo*? Similarly, *The Accused* (Jonathan Kaplan, 1988) has admirable intentions but as a film, it pales next to *Straw Dogs*.

The way the biker scene plays out, going from violence to tenderness and back to violence (as Bennie kills both men) is a pattern that is repeated often in the film. Consider the calm of the opening scene, shattered by men with guns or the romantic interlude as Bennie and Elita have a picnic, this choppily-edited but genuinely affecting scene interrupted as the car containing a couple of bounty-hunters drives slowly

Another rural idyll

past. The scenes between the lovers are some of the warm-
est in all of Peckinpah: their horseplay in bed, Bennie flicking
her with a towel until she gets up or his beaming smile when
she praises his Spanish. There are a couple of times when
Oates plays it so intensely that it is hard to watch, such as
his grudging proposal of marriage as Jerry Fielding's intrusive
score alternately evokes romance and gloomy foreboding or
the desperate look he gives Elita as she sits under the shower. Bennie can't commit to her because in Peckinpah's world,
men love death more than they love women: in an interview,
the director posed the following question:

> What is the motivation of a man who becomes a profes-
> sional soldier or an outlaw? I believe it is almost always a
> love of violence, a deep love that proves more powerful
> than the lure of money, of women and of all other pas-
> sion. (In Butler 1979: 22)

It is, no doubt, significant that Peckinpah, Oates and Bennie
all served in the military and the aforementioned doubling of
Elita and Alfredo, with Bennie telling the head that 'a friend of
ours tried to take a shower in there', is strongly suggestive of
this 'deep love'. It is that kind of movie, where a man's only
friend is a fly-blown head and nobody can get clean (notice
how Bennie doesn't say she took a shower but she 'tried to
take a shower'). The film's narrative can be regarded as one
long, slow descent to the grave: consider their journey from
the city to a plush hotel to a dump and onwards to a grave to
lots of murders to death. As Chris Petit has remarked, this is
a film completely devoid of suspense, events unfolding with
a grim inevitability. This is borne out by the aforementioned
cryptic dialogue, such as when Bennie tells Elita 'I wanna
go someplace new', or his words as he leaves El Jefe's
compound with the head, saying, 'Come on, Al, we're go-

'Come on, Al, we're going home'

ing home.' What home? The hole in the ground, where Elita waits with the rest of Al?

GETTING *ALFREDO*: PARODY AND CULT MEANING

Of course, it may all be a joke. A provocation, a parody, a piss-take. Jay Cocks, one of the few critics to give the film a positive review at the time of its release, thought it self-lacerating:

> [a] straight-faced parody ... Peckinpah means this movie to outrage; it is a kind of calculated insult mixed with generous doses of self-satire ... It is like a private bit of self-mockery, a sort of ritual of closet masochism that invites, even challenges, everyone to think the worst. Many will. That is part of what Peckinpah was after, and his success in getting it is the most disturbing element in this strange, strangled movie. (1974)

Cocks compared it to John Huston's wacky *Beat the Devil* (1954), a film so derided that even its star, Humphrey Bogart, declared that 'only phonies like it' (quoted in von Busack 1998). Cocks, who knew Peckinpah personally and was well-schooled in his work, is an extreme example of what Ernest Mathijs and Xavier Mendik refer to as the smart or avid fan. Such fans:

> Combine in-depth factual and theoretical knowledge about films with an informed understanding of narrative and stylistic sophistication. They revel in the number of references, interpretations and connections their knowledge allows them to make and by doing so they equip films with multiple subtexts. (2003a: 6)

For such a viewer, *Alfredo Garcia* is rich in allusion, full of in-jokes and autobiographical asides. For an outsider, it is easily dismissed as so much self-indulgent crap. Similarly, *Beat The Devil* is, for the avid Huston fan, a wildly funny deconstruction of the same director's *The Maltese Falcon* (1941), while to the unconverted, it is a dismally unfunny mess.

Michael Bliss suggests that Peckinpah may be 'parodying through excess' (1993: 255). Certainly, the director was perverse enough to attempt a savage satire of his own work. David Weddle relates a story from 1970. Peckinpah, increasingly frustrated by his 'Bloody Sam' image, had lost out on the chance to make a number of pet projects after *The Ballad of Cable Hogue* flopped, including adaptations of the novels *Sometimes a Great Notion* by Ken Kesey (1964), *Play it as it Lays* (1970) by Joan Didion and *Deliverance* (1970) by James Dickey (Peckinpah was Dickey's choice to adapt his novel, as the author considered both men to be 'doing the same thing ... We're trying to give them things they can't forget' (quoted in Sragow 2000b)). He had reluctantly agreed to direct an adaptation of Gordon Williams' pulpy novel, *The Seige of Trencher's Farm* (1969), which would become *Straw*

Dogs. (The director was no fan of the source novel, saying 'it makes you want to drown in your own puke', while Williams said of Peckinpah, 'the man was sick' (quoted in Taylor 2003).) Before leaving for the UK, Peckinpah sat up drinking with a friend and lamenting his lot. 'All right', Weddle quotes him as saying. 'They want to see brains flying out? I'll give them brains flying out' (1995: 20). It may well be that he intended *Alfredo Garcia* to be another such provocation, a scrappy, booze-sodden death trip from the Old Iguana. If so, it worked, with the response to the film, as noted earlier, being almost overwhelmingly negative. Even its defenders have to concede that it is a hard film to like: it seems to wallow in the degradation the director's critics always accused him of peddling. In this respect, it is reminiscent of Hitchcock's *Frenzy*, of which Peckinpah spoke admiringly: 'I am not a Hitchcock fanatic but all the same one has to admit that he knows how to render tangible … human suffering' (quoted in Prince 1998: 223). *Frenzy* was Hitchcock's penultimate film and he took full advantage of the greater freedoms afforded filmmakers in the early part of the 1970s, offering up a graphic rape/murder which gives full vent to the kind of vicious, kinky misogyny many had detected in his earlier work. Even his many admirers are conflicted about the sequence: for Robin Wood it is the film's 'most impressive, and most profoundly disturbing, scene' (1991: 345), while Donald Spoto regarded it as both a 'personal self-disclosure of the director's angriest and most violent desires' and 'one of the most repellent examples of a detailed murder in the history of film' (1983: 513). The blatant nastiness of *Frenzy* seems intended, in part, to provoke, perhaps even to disgust, but it also fits nicely into the director's body of work. The ageing Hitchcock returned to London after many years in America and this story of a serial killer stalking the capital echoes *The Lodger* (1926), his first thriller (and first hit).

The setting of *Frenzy* was seen by many as hopelessly out of date, 'wildly anachronistic … providing merely a tourist's eye view of modern London' (Spoto 1983: 518): indeed, if Spoto is to be believed, screenwriter Anthony Shaffer 'and the cast were expressing similar judgements' (ibid). But this is to misjudge Hitchcock and his ambitious attempt to make a film that, in John Orr's words, 'simultaneously evoked the London to which he returned in 1972 and the London he had left in 1939, the 1970s and the 1930s within a single film' (2005: 68). Orr compares *Frenzy* favourably to *Blue Velvet* and his praise is echoed by other recent writers on this most discussed of directors: 'a Hitchcock travelogue of London but also a personal scrapbook of memories' (McGilligan 2003: 699) and 'a pastiche and reprise of his work … and a coded autobiography … his most insidiously personal film, the Catholic director's final confession' (Jones 1999). *Frenzy*, then, can be regarded as Hitchcock's *Alfredo Garcia*: a fitting summation of and comment on his body of work which was misunderstood and often derided; a film that sets out to turn off as many as it entertains; a complex, ambitious work which many critics just failed to get, seeing it as proof that a once-great talent had lost his touch (in Hitchcock's case, through illness and age; in Peckinpah's case, through alcohol and self-indulgence). The relationship *Frenzy* has to Hitchcock's filmography is reflected in the way *Alfredo Garcia* seems to extend, reference and even sum up Peckinpah's own authorial concerns. His first film, the aforementioned *The Deadly Companions*, is about a journey undertaken with a rotting body and *Pat Garrett and Billy the Kid* appears to end at the point that *Alfredo Garcia* begins. The director himself appears as Will the coffin-maker, 'a sad dealer in death' (Prince 1998: 198), whom Garrett meets as he makes his way across the street to kill his former friend, Billy. Magnificently grizzled, bitter and mournful, Will/Peckinpah (I am not sure that we are supposed to make a distinction), after calling Garrett 'a chicken-shit, badge-wearing sonofabitch', asks him:

> You know what I'm going to do? I'm going to put everything I own here right here [in a coffin]. And I'm going to bury it in the ground and then I'm going to leave the territory.

So a year or so later some poor bastard like Bennie can try and dig it up? *Alfredo Garcia* seems to continue this bleak climax more than just tonally. Peckinpah pouring scorn on one of his many alter egos serves to prepare us for the suffering he inflicts on Bennie.

A rotting head, pubic lice, grave-robbing, 21 murders … it's as if the director is serving up a venomous riposte to his many critics. The sweat and the booze, the crabs popped between fingernails, the casual cruelty, breaking bones and rotting flesh. It isn't hard to see how many viewers feel sullied by the film, feel that this boozy, disjointed *Grand Guignol* is like a physical assault. The whole thing, the grim events and the execution of it, could be another manifestation of Peckinpah's self-destructive streak, remarked upon earlier in this chapter. Drugs, drink, violence and a lack of diplomacy are not uncommon traits in artists (on the contrary: they often seem to be a requirement for the job). But what is unusual is the way this self-destructiveness would extend to the director's work. When dealing with projects he found unworthy of his talents, he often employed various devices to create an ironic distance from the material. Sometimes, this could look an awful lot like sabotage. In his 'whoring' assignments, such as *The Getaway* (his biggest hit), *The Killer Elite* (a spy thriller with added kung fu) and *The Osterman Weekend* (a confused Robert Ludlum adaptation), he encouraged the actors to improvise and played up plot holes and illogicalities, satirising and sometimes ridiculing his material. For example, he shot an alternative ending for *The Killer Elite*, where a dead character was resurrected, and tried to insert unfunny one-liners and comments (including, unwisely, some about the studio, MGM). The star of the film, James Caan, remarked that Peckinpah 'had private jokes in the film for twenty or thirty of his pals' (in Fine 2005: 284), the director taking the self-mockery of *Alfredo Garcia* to an absurd level.

There are a lot of things in *Alfredo Garcia* that I suspect are supposed to be funny, although they often come over as unpleasant (Bennie's crabs) or weird (when the Garcia family corner Bennie and the bus passes between them, the Mexicans exchange waves with the passengers on the bus). There is often a tension between passionate intensity (the performances of Oates and Vega, the overwhelming Fielding score) and detached irony (Gig Young's smirks, the stiffness of Helmut Dantine, the slapdash shoot-outs). Certainly, as a man, Peckinpah seems to have embodied both these qualities: on the one hand, he would lament 'I get into many problems, I drink too much and I get into too many fights' (in Bryson 2008: 141), yet he also claimed to 'regard everything with irony, including the face I see in the mirror when I wake up in the morning' (in Seydor 1980: 228). All of these weird devices, the echoing, the jokes, the contrivances, combined with the excessive *mise-en-scène*, create a distance for the viewer. What could be seen as lazy or corny can also be regarded as providing a layer of irony, a kind of critical commentary on the action. Like the cartoons and spiders at the opening of *Persona* or the phoney back-projections in *Marnie*, the jarring elements in *Alfredo Garcia*, whether employed by design or through carelessness, make the whole experience an unnerving one. Phil Nugent suggests that Peckinpah's sloppiness is a deliberate strategy, saying that the viewer has to wonder 'if Peckinpah's message is that not only can the world no longer support any kind of nobility, it can't even justi-fy basic competence, not even from one of the world's great-est moviemakers'. He goes on to consider how 'the crafts-manship on display seems to disintegrate before a viewer's eyes' (2005). Nugent's comments bring to mind Umberto Eco's comments (1986) on *Casablanca* as cult movie, with its 'glorious ricketiness' and 'incoherence' (although if Eco considers *Casablanca* as rickety and incoherent, I would love to know what he thinks of *Alfredo Garcia*).

By the end of the film, we are left in no doubt that none of it means anything. After Bennie hands over the head, El Jefe orders his men to 'throw it to the pigs'. All that killing and for what? Pigshit. After he kills El Jefe, Bennie walks out carry-ing the head and leaving the suitcase full of money behind, going back almost as an afterthought to collect it. This bleak denouement is even more deflating than the empty gold sack skewered on a cactus in *The Treasure of the Sierra Madre*, the sound of bitter laughter in that film replaced here by the rattle of machine-gun fire. Is this the reason the film seems to peter out, to end in so anti-climactic a fashion? Does this explain the shifts in tone and logic, the grainy cinematogra-phy and the muddy sound, the slapdash slo-mo? Does none of it mean anything, onscreen or off?

4

'YOU TOO ARE WRONG. DEAD WRONG': PLACING *ALFREDO*

'PURE PECKINPAH' AND CULT PURITY

It is tempting to say *Bring Me the Head of Alfredo Garcia* is a unique film. But isn't that par for the course for cult films? Certainly, as suggested earlier, it is in a tradition of films that have achieved cult status by being the misunderstood or ignored bastard offspring of important directors. Indeed, it was Robert Altman who said of his films, 'it's like your own children … we tend to love our least successful children the most' (quoted in Mondello 2006). These words will make sense to any fan of neglected works by acclaimed filmmakers. (This is a strand within cultdom to rival the 'one-hit wonders', the directors who leave only one film, such as Charles Laughton with his weird and beautiful *The Night of the Hunter* or James William Guercio, the record producer whose sole directorial outing is the striking *Electra Glide in Blue* (1973).) Of course, Altman's words can also be applied to cult movies per se, a whole canon of much-loved, least successful children.

As the previous chapters have demonstrated, *Alfredo Garcia* also follows a well-worn path to cultdom by virtue of being a critical and commercial flop, rediscovered by successive generations of fans. But I think its importance is greater than that. Consider *The Wild Bunch*, one of the unquestioned masterpieces of the American cinema, with its excellent ensemble playing, innovative use of multi-camera set-ups and skillfully mounted action scenes. Compared to this, on many levels, *Alfredo Garcia* can be regarded as a disaster, the squandering of a major talent. But look closer. It has a strange appeal, this lyrical car crash of a film. It's hopeless, both on and offscreen; an ugly, sour tale that plays out like a nightmare. There are times when Peckinpah almost seems to encourage us to walk out of the cinema: Benny dousing his crab-infested crotch, anointing Al's head with drink, waking up buried in a grave alongside his dead girlfriend. Even if you close your eyes, the soundtrack is still heady stuff: the loud snap of a pregnant woman's bone breaking, the buzz of flies around the head, all that gunfire. Certainly, the film was, and still is, a huge turn-off to many. But this strange mix of the poetic and the hideous is as compelling as it is off-putting. While so many cult films are mutilated before release or exist in different forms (*Performance*, *The Wicker Man*, *Blade Runner* (Ridley Scott, 1982), *Donnie Darko* (Richard Kelly, 2001)), *Alfredo Garcia* stands out as the only film Peckinpah made without interference. Whereas *Straw Dogs* was censored, *Cross of Iron* had its budget slashed mid-shoot, *The Getaway* was re-edited and re-scored and *Major Dundee*, *The Wild Bunch* and *Pat Garrett and Billy the Kid* were mutilated, it is only *Alfredo Garcia* that can be regarded as 'pure Peckinpah'.

This notion of 'purity', what Walter Benjamin (2003) terms the 'aura of uniqueness' possessed by a work of art, is an important one to the cultist. Purity in art is a nebulous concept and a deeply problematic one when applied to film: are the mainstream films of Steven Spielberg, say, less pure than the exploitation films of Jess Franco? If so, then why? Yet this search for the genuine, the real and the undiluted is surely one of the factors behind such popular cult fare as mondo movies, porn and splatter films. The following comments typify this desire for purity:

There was a certain purity to its head-on violence (BC, 20/01/2009) on *A'l'intérieur/Inside* (Alexandre Bustillo/ Julien Maury, 2007) at ART.CULT. (Lee 2009)

For the cult movie enthusiast, these films, from Ed Wood's to Mario Bava's to John Waters' have a purity and an authenticity not found in their mainstream counterparts. (Sherman 2009)

Despite *Army of Darkness* being self-aware or geared towards a certain audience, it still maintains a purity created by Raimi's boyish experiments and silliness. (James, 5/11/2008) at Cult Media Studies.

The strange space that *Alfredo Garcia* occupies in Peckinpah's oeuvre, its inscrutability and scrappiness, means it resonates beyond other (better?) films by the same director, its flaws and faults unashamedly foregrounded. A large part of the appeal for many fans is the sense that it is a film unrestrained by standards of taste, talent, competence and even sanity.

Yet still, as with so many cult films, rumours swirl around it, talk of cuts and missing scenes: there are Internet discussions about the abrupt ending and whispers of 'the necrophilia scene' where Benny has sex with the dead Elita in Alfredo's grave. On IMDb, reviewer Steve Fischer from New York City relates how he:

saw the film in Manhattan on the day it opened so many years ago. After the reviews came out, the studio immediately pulled the prints from the theatres and cut the most CRUCIAL scene in the film. The original release contained a scene wherein upon discovering his lover dead, the Warren Oates character makes love to her corpse … It is in this moment that he slips into madness. If you watch the film again, note the transition from the 'pre-grave' character and the 'post-grave' one. (Also note the somewhat disjointed transition from his holding his dead lover in his arms, to his leaving the graveyard.) (Posted on 16 January, 2002)

This may be persuasive to some, and Kathleen Murphy and Richard Jameson have acknowledged that Bennie's 'movements grotesquely suggest a sexual dalliance' (1981: 48), but I think these stories circulate in large part due to the film's elliptical (some would say botched) structure and what may be, as we have seen in the previous chapter, a deliberate strategy of 'anti-pleasure'. There isn't another film like it: John Patterson put it well when he said, 'they really don't make 'em like this anymore. Truth is, they never did. This is the only one' (2008). But that doesn't stop a small army of acolytes and imitators doing their best to channel the shade of Peckinpah: 'has there ever been a director whose style has been so shamelessly, and shallowly, lifted?', adding how his 'legion of imitators … mistook the bloodshed for bloodlust, deep melancholy for cheap comedy' (Hultkrans 2008).

ALFREDO'S CHILDREN

The Robert Rodriguez/Frank Miller neo-noir *Sin City* (2005) is a good example of this, containing an explicit homage to *Alfredo Garcia*, as a character drives along, conversing with a severed head. But this reference sits uneasily alongside the film's macho men, gangsters and Bruce Willis. Sure, there is violence and psychosis in Peckinpah's film but there is also sentimentality and romance, great delicacy and wide streaks of self-lacerating neurosis. This is so often the way that filmmakers summon up the spirit of the Old Iguana, substituting slow-motion violence and would-be machismo for his dyspeptic, brutal poetry. Although they have their defenders, would anybody seriously consider John Woo (*The Killer* (1989)), Luc Besson (*Léon* (1994)) or Robert Rodriguez (*Desperado* (1995)) in the same class as Peckinpah? Guns, male bonding and Mexico do not an *Alfredo Garcia* make. Far more impressive was *The Three Burials of Melquiades Estrada* (2005), the directorial debut of actor Tommy Lee Jones (whose grizzled visage and laconic delivery make him one of the few contemporary actors who would be at home in the Peckinpah stock company). This tale of a ranch-hand (Jones) who transports the body of his eponymous friend across the border for burial, accompanied by his killer, cannot help but recall Peckinpah. It was, therefore, no surprise when the director/star confessed to having watched *Alfredo Garcia* repeatedly ('about 15 times and I love Peckinpah's work' (in Dupont 2005)). While the film heaps a series of indignities on the decomposing Estrada (including an anti-freeze injection and face-eating ants), the end offers a touching redemption far from Peckinpah's freeze-framed gun barrel. *Bring Me the Head of Alfredo Garcia* is certainly an ordeal, all that cynicism and flop sweat, self-pity and disgust. But it's a very different kind of experience than that offered by horror films like *Henry: Portrait of a Serial Killer* (John MacNaughton, 1986) or *Seul contre tous* (*I Stand Alone*, Gaspar Noé, 1998). The nihilism of MacNaughton and Noé is so aggressive, it's almost invigorating, lashings of dread and murder observed by a camera that pointedly refuses to look away. There is nihilism in Peckinpah's film but it's a kind of romantic nihilism, a wounded, tequila-soaked bitterness. In 2002, MacNaughton listed Peckinpah's film as one of his ten favourites, in the Best Film Poll run by *Sight & Sound* magazine. Similarly, a *Time Out* poll in 1995 to celebrate the centenary of cinema saw *Alfredo Garcia* feature in the top ten of Takeshi Kitano, the Japanese game-show host/author/painter/actor/director. This should come as no surprise to anyone familiar with Kitano's films such as *Sono otoko, kyôbô ni tsuki* (*Violent Cop*, 1989), *Sonatine* (1993) and *Hana-bi* (1997), with their melancholy portraits of taciturn, violent men.

I don't know if it's any measure of the off-putting content or the brilliance of its title that makes most of the homages to Peckinpah's film puns or word-plays. Aside from the examples mentioned in an earlier chapter, there is *Bring Me the Head of Dobie Gillis* (Stanley Z. Cherry, 1988) and the little-seen *Bring Me the Head of Charlie Brown* (Jim Reardon, 1986), the latter dedicated to Peckinpah. There is also 'Bring Me the Head of Boba Fett', the pilot of the animated show *Welcome to Eltingville* (2002). 2009 will see the first production of a German play by Werner Fritsch, *Bring Mir Den Kopf von Kurt Cobain* (*Bring Me the Head of Kurt Cobain*).

There are more substantial *Alfredo Garcia* echoes in *The Mexican* (Gore Verbinsky, 2001), which substitutes A-list stars (Brad Pitt and Julia Roberts) and a pair of antique pistols for Warren Oates and a head in a sack, as well as in *The Way of the Gun* (Christopher McQuarrie, 2000) where Ryan Phillippe and Benicio Del Toro play losers who end up in a south of the border bullet-fest. Indeed, Del Toro is an avowed Peckinpah fan, turning up in the documentary feature *Sam Peckinpah's West: Legacy of a Hollywood Renegade*. There have been rumours for some time that the actor would take the lead in a remake of *Alfredo Garcia* (possibly due to him being one of the few actors in these Botoxed times who looks knackered enough to play Bennie) but, at the time of writing, nothing substantial. It goes without saying that re-making a film that is so defiantly a Peckinpah film *sans* the Old Iguana is a stupid idea. But that doesn't mean someone won't try it. As mainstream films become more and more expensive to make, name recognition is one way of bringing in an audience. No matter that a film has little relation to its source material (the *Mission: Impossible* trilogy, 1996, 2000, 2006), or happens to be a lousy/pointless re-tread (the termi-nally stupid 're-imagining' of *Planet of the Apes* (Tim Burton, 2001), *Alfie* (Charles Shyer, 2004), *Starsky and Hutch* (Todd Phillips, 2004)). So why should the Old Barnacle be immune to this phenomenon? There have been reports of a remake of *The Wild Bunch* and a re-working of *Straw Dogs* with Edward Norton in the Dustin Hoffman role and Rod Lurie as the direc-tor. In interviews, Lurie has (unwittingly) put his finger on why Peckinpah's films are so striking and why remaking them is an exercise in redundancy. Calling the film 'very imperfect' and Peckinpah's direction of it 'a little lazy', Lurie 'plans im-provements' to the original: 'It was pretty much killed by a two-second moment on screen where his wife is being raped and she smiles. That was the end of that movie. You can be certain that she's not going to be smiling in the rape in my film' (quoted in Walsh 2007). Does Lurie (the director of *The Contender* (2000)) really think that ironing out ambigui-ties and letting an audience off the hook can be regarded as 'an improvement'? Much of the strength of Peckinpah's work lies in its ability to trouble and disturb with its myriad complexities and grey areas, its worrying undertows.

The television drama, *Low Winter Sun* (2006), directed by Adrian Shergold, is a bleak slice of Tartan Noir that con-tains (unconscious?) echoes of Peckinpah's film, with a plot revolving around a suitcase full of money and a severed head in a bag. In one scene, a character (played by Brian

McCardie) plays piano, wearing a blood-stained light suit, à la Bennie. One contributor to the *Film Comment* website sees Peckinpah's influence in the best films of 2007. Discussing *No Country For Old Men* (Joel Coen), *Zodiac* (David Fincher) and *There Will Be Blood* (Paul Thomas Anderson), Adam Protextor observes that 'collectively, they represent a return to Peckinpah's Man – an independent man of honour and violence who cannot function in normal society' (2008). Indeed, it's possible to see a through-line from *The Treasure of the Sierra Madre* to *Alfredo Garcia* and *Chinatown* (Roman Polanski, 1974) and ending at *There Will Be Blood*, all films about greed and the monsters it makes of men. Perhaps the most fitting homage to Peckinpah's film is the recurring one in *Deadwood* (2004–06), the brutal western series created by David Chase for the US television network HBO. This show, with its complex tale of a muddy, bloody Frontier town peopled by whores and killers, has a strong cast of grizzled veterans such as Brad Dourif, Keith Carradine and Ian McShane, and is authentically Peckinpavian. The character of murderous saloon owner Al Swearengen (McShane) keeps the head of an Indian in a box in his office and regularly regales it with boozy soliloquies. This is a nice nod to the Old Barnacle, particularly so when one considers how the savage world on show in *Deadwood* shares much with the world of *Alfredo Garcia*, with brutality, death and pitch-black humour filtered through a haze of liquor.

CONCLUSION

In some ways, having spent some time writing the book you are reading, I want to cop-out and conclude that it is an impossible film to really assess. This is partly because I do not think Peckinpah entirely knew what he was doing and partly because like all truly great films, it seems to change and grow with every viewing. It is both brilliant and awful and, as such, asks us to reassess what these terms mean. In the same way, it asks us to consider notions of authorship, all those romantic views of the artist as a misunderstood, self-destructive visionary: indeed, Peckinpah fits that template better than most, a violent, paranoid alcoholic whose unwillingness to compromise ended up destroying his once-promising career. It raises questions about setting 'quality cinema' against a kind of unmediated self-expression/indulgence. How much do we value notions of 'quality' and what happens when these notions come into conflict with art, particularly repulsive, inconsistent or just plain shoddy art? How useful is Bertolt Brecht's idea of rejecting the 'well-made' in this case? Do we come out of *Alfredo Garcia* reflecting on the violence of the film, the ugliness, the tenderness of it? Or is the ineptitude of its execution and the bleakness of tone just a huge turn-off? How enervating can a film be when it seems to revel in the fact that nothing matters, not love, not honour, not money, not film?

To many, Peckinpah's film is a defiantly ugly work, a confused and confusing film that gets under the skin of those who see it in a way that 'better' films could never hope to do. Perhaps its lasting legacy is that it represents a kind of untramelled free expression, an autobiographical vomiting up of neuroses and bile from a director who has come to represent a very personal type of filmmaking, one that we see fewer and fewer examples of with every passing year. A film so naked, raw and personal that even three decades later, viewers are thrilled and moved, or they recoil in embarrassment, disgust or loathing. In 1972, Peckinpah gave an in-depth interview to *Playboy* magazine's William Murray. The director's lengthy response to Murray's question 'when you say that someone is a real man, what do you mean by it?', included the following:

It's the ultimate test. You either compromise to the point where it destroys you or you stand up and say 'fuck off'. It's amazing how few people will do that. (In Murray 2008: 108)

Bring Me the Head of Alfredo Garcia should be regarded as Sam Peckinpah's glorious, furious fuck off.

NOTES

1   I have not forgotten the enormous influence that German cinema had on Hollywood from the 1920s through to (at the very least) the 1940s, influencing the visual style of genres including horror, the gangster film and film noir. But these techniques were brought over by the filmmakers themselves: directors like F. W. Murnau, Ernst Lubitsch, Edgar J. Ulmer and Billy Wilder and cinematographers like Karl Freund.

2   I have been informed by series co-editor Jamie Sexton that Guy Ritchie was similarly parodied on *The Adam and Joe Show* (1996–97). However, given that the same show also spoofed Larry Clark (staging his *Kids* (1996) with a cast of cuddly toys), it is safe to say that their parodies are aimed at a niche, cine-literate audience.

3   The popular television show *Starsky and Hutch* (1975–79) is a vivid example of the homoerotic nature of the buddy cycle. The ´disclaimer´ in this case is the androgynous, silk-scarved Huggie Bear, played by Antonio Fargas (although Fargas was ´out-camped´ by the rapper Snoop Dogg in the otherwise forgettable 2004 film version). The show´s iconic credit sequence includes Hutch (David Soul) watching a (female) stripper only to be distracted by Starsky (Paul Michael Glaser) blowing in his ear, Starsky swooning only to be caught by Hutch and a climactic explosion that causes both men to end up in each other´s arms. The freeze-frame that follows fixes the partners mid-embrace.

BIBLIOGRAPHY

Anderson, J. M. (2005) 'Bring Me the Head of Alfredo Garcia', Combustible Celluloid, http://tinyurl.com/35cxl4r (accessed 14 February 2008).

Andrews, N. (2009) 'Sex, Tempts and Redemption', Financial Times, http://tinyurl.com/3ybk6uy (accessed 16 March 2009).

Anon. (1994) 'Gig Young's Parting Shot', EntertainmentWeekly.com, http://tinyurl.com/35kqjp6 (accessed 10 October 2008).

Atkinson, M. (2000) 'Duels in the Sun', Village Voice, http://tinyurl.com/38vlwzn (accessed 14 February 2008).

____ (2005) 'Head Hunter: Peckinpah's Anarchic Nixon-Era Neo-Noir', Village Voice, http://tinyurl.com/355z92u (accessed 14 February 2008).

Balz, A. (2006) 'Bring Me the Head of Alfredo Garcia', Not Coming to a Cinema Near You, http://tinyurl.com/2wx2ld2 (accessed 10 October 2007).

Barker, M. (2006) 'Loving and Hating Straw Dogs: The Meanings of Audience Responses to a Controversial Film – Part 2: Rethinking Straw Dogs as a Film', Particip@tions, Vol. 3, http://tinyurl.com/2wbq8z7 (accessed 13 July 2009).

Barr, C. (1972) 'Straw Dogs, A Clockwork Orange and the critics', Screen, Summer, 17–31.

Benjamin, W. (2003 [1935]) 'The Work of Art in the Age of Mechanical Reproduction', in E. Mathijs and X. Mendik (eds) The Cult Film Reader. New York: McGraw Hill Open University Press, 29–40.

Biskind, P. (1998) Easy Riders Raging Bulls. London: Bloomsbury.

Bliss, M. (1993) Justified Lives: Morality and Narrative in the Films of Sam Peckinpah. Carbondale and Edwardsville: Southern Illinois University Press.

Bomar, A. F and A. J. Warren (1981) 'Warren Oates interview', Oates Articles and Interviews, http://www.geocities.com/Hollywood/Location/9947/articles.html (accessed 18 May 2008).

Boone, S. (2005) 'There's nothing sacred about a hole in the ground. Or you. Or me', *Big Media Vandalism*, http://tinyurl.com/38hcjyc (accessed 10 October 2008).

Brottman, M. (2008) 'Cult Films: B Movies and Trash', *Film Reference*, http://tinyurl.com/37zwoqq (accessed 13 June 2009).

Bryson, J. (2008 [1974]) 'The Wild Bunch in New York', in K. J. Hayes (ed.) *Sam Peckinpah Interviews*. Jackson: University of Mississippi Press, 137–44.

Butler, T. (1979) *Crucified Heroes. The Films of Sam Peckinpah*. London: Gordon Fraser.

Cagin, S. and P. Dray (1994) *Born to Be Wild. Hollywood and the Sixties Generation*. Florida: Coyote.

Canby, V. (1974) '*Bring Me the Head of Alfredo Garcia*', *Variety.com*, http://tinyurl.com/37tapff (accessed 24 June 2008).

Chaffin-Quiray, G. (2007) 'Sam Peckinpah', in S. J. Schneider (ed.) *501 Movie Directors*. London: Quintessence, 282–3.

Chopra-Gant, M. (2008) *Cinema and History: The Telling of Stories*. London: Wallflower Press.

Clark, G. (2008) '*Bring Me the Head of Alfredo Garcia*', *The Spinning Image*, http://tinyurl.com/397w8tg (accessed 24 June 2008).

Cocks, J. (1974) 'Horseless Headsman: *Bring Me the Head of Alfredo Garcia*', *Time*, http://tinyurl.com/295pow7 (accessed 25 August 2008).

Cohan, S. and I. R. Hark (1997) 'Introduction', in S. Cohen and I. R. Hark (eds) *The Road Movie Book*. London and New York: Routledge, 1–14.

Collings, A. (2008) 'The Quietus Looks Back At Alex Cox's Moviedrome', *The Quietus*, http://tinyurl.com/297arxh (accessed 2 April 2009).

Combs, R. (1975) '*Bring Me the Head of Alfredo Garcia*', *Sight & Sound*, 44, 2, 121.

_____ (1985) 'Top Ten', in P. Hardy (ed) *The Aurum Film Encyclopedia: Horror*. London: Aurum Press, 397.

Corrigan, T. (1991) *A Cinema Without Walls: Movies and Culture After Vietnam*. London: Routledge.

Cox, A. (2006) 'A Bullet in the Back', *Guardian*, http://tinyurl.com/3al3z4d (accessed 19 February 2009).

Davison, P. (2007) 'Obituary: Alex Phillips Jnr.', *Independent*, http://tinyurl.com/35xsnrz (accessed 10 October 2008).

Delapa, T. (2004) '*Bring Me the Head of Alfredo Garcia*', *Rotten Tomatoes*, http://tinyurl.com/3a4hf4j (accessed 10 October 2007).

Dupont, J. (2005) 'The Faces of Tommy Lee Jones', *New York Times*, http://tinyurl.com/3a5s7f4 (accessed 19 February 2009).

Ebert, R. (2001 [1974]) 'Great Movies: *Bring Me the Head of Alfredo Garcia*', http://tinyurl.com/e5l2y (accessed 10 October 2007).

____ (2003) 'Great Movies: *The Treasure of the Sierra Madre*', http://tinyurl.com/39ln9f (accessed 26 April 2008).

Eco, U. (1986) 'Cult Movies and Intertextual Collage', *Travels in Hyper-Reality*. London: Picador, 197– 211.

Elley, D. (1975) '*Bring Me the Head of Alfredo Garcia*', *Films and Filming*, 21, 5, 35.

English, R. (2006) 'Guns and Tequila. The Life and Times of Sam Peckinpah', *Modern Drunkard Magazine*, http://tinyurl.com/33h2km5 (accessed 10 October 2008).

Fine, M. (2005) *Bloody Sam. The Life And Films Of Sam Peckinpah*. New York: Hyperion.

Fitzgerald, S. (2003) '*Bring Me the Head of Alfredo Garcia*', *The 70s Movies Rewind*, http://70s.fast-rewind.com (accessed 10 October 2007).

French, P. (2007) 'How violent taboos were blown away', *Observer*, http://tinyurl.com/3axgbxx (accessed 13 June 2009).

____ (2009) '*Bring Me the Head of Alfredo Garcia*', *Observer*, http://tinyurl.com/7lvz2y (accessed 10 January 2009).

Garcia, A. (2004–06) *Fauxhunter*, http://www.fauxhunter.co.uk (accessed 10 October 2007).

Grobel, L. (1989) *The Hustons*. New York: Avon Books.

Hayes, K. J. (ed.) (2008) *Sam Peckinpah Interviews*. Jackson: University of Mississippi Press.

Hultkrans, A. (2008) 'Truest Grit', *Artforum*, http://tinyurl.com/38rqqxe (accessed 10 January 2009).

Jameson, R. T. and K. Murphy (1981) '*Bring Me the Head of Alfredo Garcia*', *Film Comment*, 17,1, 44–8.

Jancovich, M., A. L. Reboll, J. Stringer and A. Willis (eds) (2003) *Defining Cult Movies: The Cultural Politics of Oppositional Taste*. Manchester University Press.

Jenson, L. (2008 [1970]) 'Sam and Stella', in K. J. Hayes (ed.) *Sam Peckinpah Interviews*. Jackson: University of Mississippi Press, 62–81.

Jon (2007) '*Bring Me the Head of Alfredo Garcia*', *Projections: What Latin America Tells Us At The Movies*,http://tinyurl.com/373dv3c (accessed 10 October 2008).

Jones, J. (1999) 'The body in the river', *Guardian*, http://tinyurl.com/34vb22j (accessed 10 October 2008).

Kael, P. (1999) 'A Glorious High', *Austin Chronicle*, http://tinyurl.com/347f8ap (accessed 10 October 2007).

Kermode, M. (2003) 'A wild bunch in Cornwall', *Observer*, http://www.tinyurl.com/3x6yws2 (accessed 19 February 2009).

Kerstein, B. (2006) 'The Last Man: An Epitaph for Sam Peckinpah', *Senses of Cinema*, http://tinyurl.com/3am788e (accessed 10 October 2008).

Kolker, R. (2000) *A Cinema of Loneliness: Penn, Stone, Kubrick, Scorsese, Spielberg, Altman*. Oxford: Oxford University Press.

Koweski, K. (2006) 'Guerilla Poetics Project: Outlaw Poetry…', http://guerillapoetics.blogspot.com/2006/07/outlaw-poetry.html (accessed 26 April 2008).

Kraniauskas, J. (1993) 'Stepping Over the Border', *Sight & Sound*, 3, 6, 32–3.

Krohn, B. (1992) '*Full Metal Jacket*', *The Kubrick Site*, http://tinyurl.com/36ap3xp (accessed 26 April 2008).

Lee, N. (2009) 'The Best Films of 2008', *ART:CULT*, http://tinyurl.com/2vdt5cc/ (accessed 13 May 2009).

Lester, J. (1998) '*Bring Me the Head of Alfredo Garcia*', *LazyBastard.com*, http://tinyurl.com/37h25y5 (accessed 10 October 2007).

Linklater, R. (2008) 'Things I Love About *Two-Lane Blacktop*', *Alamo Drafthouse Cinema*, July, http://tinyurl.com/32e9jk5 (accessed 14 September 2008).

Long, P. (2009) '*Bring Me the Head of Alfredo Garcia*', *Electric Sheep*, 23, http://tinyurl.com/2wxmxqm/ (accessed 10 January 2009).

Lons (2005) '*Bring Me the Head of Alfredo Garcia*', *Crushed by Inertia*, http://tinyurl.com/2v6y6qw (accessed 10 October 2007).

Luck, R. (2000) 'The Brown Dirt Cowboy', *tedstrong.com*, http://tinyurl.com/2vdwqo8 (accessed 10 October 2008).

Macklin, F. Anthony (2008 [1976]) 'Mort Sahl Called Me a 1939 American', in K. J. Hayes (ed.) *Sam Peckinpah Interviews*. Jackson: University of Mississippi Press, 145–57.

Madsen, A. (1974) 'Peckinpah in Mexico', *Sight & Sound*, 43, 2, 91.

Maltin, L. (1998) *Leonard Maltin's Movie & Video Guide 1999*. London and New York: Penguin Books.

Mathijs, E. (2008) *David Cronenberg: From Baron of Blood to Cultural Hero*. London: Wallflower Press.

Mathijs, E. and X. Mendik (2003a) 'Editorial Introduction: What is Cult Film?', *The Cult Film Reader*. New York: McGraw Hill Open University Press, 1–11.

____ (2003b) 'Section 1: The Concepts of Cult. Introduction', *The Cult Film Reader*. New York: McGraw Hill Open University Press, 15–24.

McGilligan, P. (2003) *Alfred Hitchcock: A Life in Darkness and Light*. Chichester: Wiley.

Medved, H., M. Medved and R. Dreyfuss (1978) *The Fifty Worst Movies of all Time*. New York: Warner.

Miller, M. C. (1975) 'In Defense of Sam Peckinpah', *Film Quarterly*, 28, 3, 2–17.

Mondello, B. (2006) 'Film World Mourns Director Robert Altman', *NPR*, http://tinyurl.com/36jv8v6 (accessed 10 October 2008).

Moody, R. (2009) 'Inside the Head of Sam Peckinpah', *Guardian*, http://tinyurl.com/32n2z7h (accessed 10 January 2009).

Moore, T. (2006) 'Guerilla Poetics Project: Outlaw Poetry...', http://guerillapoetics.blogspot.com/2006/07/outlaw-poetry.html (accessed 26 April 2008).

Murphy, K. (1984) 'Sam Peckinpah: No Bleeding Heart', *Film Comment*, 21, 2, 74–5.

Murray, G. (2002) 'Great Directors: Sam Peckinpah', *Senses of Cinema*, http://tinyurl.com/cgr3kr (accessed 10 October 2007).

Murray, W. (2008 [1972]) 'Playboy Interview: Sam Peckinpah', in K. J. Hayes (ed.) *Sam Peckinpah Interviews*. Jackson: University of Mississippi Press, 96–120.

Naremore, J. (2007) *On Kubrick*. London: British Film Institute.

Nashawaty, C. (2006) 'The DVD Insomniac: Wild Oates', *EntertainmentWeekly.com*, http://tinyurl.com/33dw92a (accessed 1 December 2008).

Neumaier, J. (2004) 'Warren Oates Living on the Edge', *tedstrong.com*, http://tinyurl.com/35d65eq (accessed 26 April 2008).

Newman, K. (2009) '*Bring Me the Head of Alfredo Garcia*', *Times Online*, http://tinyurl.com/34ftqrx (accessed 16 March 2009).

Newman, M. Z. (2008) 'Notes on Cult Films and New Media Technology', *Zigzigger*, http://tinyurl.com/32x7fqj (accessed 2 April 2009).

Nugent, P. (2005) '*Bring Me the Head of Alfredo Garcia*', *The High Hat*, http://tinyurl.com/32j7qno (accessed 23 April 2007).

Orecklin, M. (1998) 'From Rosebud to Roadhouse', *Time*, http://tinyurl.
com/ycaxxus (accessed 26 April 2008).

Orr, J. (2005) *Hitchcock and 20th Century Cinema*. London: Wallflower
Press.

Ostrand, M. (2006) 'Emilio Fernandez: One of a Kind', *Mexico Connect*,
http://tinyurl.com/39hf89b (accessed 10 October 2007).

Pallot, J. *et al.* (1994) *The Third Virgin Film Guide*. London: Virgin.

Patterson, J. (2008) 'The Pick of Peckinpah', *Guardian*, http://tinyurl.
com/2vmqmej (accessed 10 January 2009).

Petit, C. (1998) '*Bring Me the Head of Alfredo Garcia*', *Time Out Film
Guide*. London: Time Out Group, 28–9.

Pierson, M. H. (1999) 'Warren Oates. 1928–1982', *tedstrong.com*,
http://tinyurl.com/32w3nlk (accessed 10 October 2008).

Poague, L. (2005) 'Poague on Wounded Cinema', *Screening the Past*,
http://tinyurl.com/38fqreb (accessed 14 February 2008).

Porter, E. (2009) '*Bring Me the Head of Alfredo Garcia*', *Sunday Times*,
http://tinyurl.com/37cjlwa (accessed 19 February 2008).

Prince, S. (1998) *Sam Peckinpah and the Rise of Ultraviolent Movies*.
Austin: University of Texas Press.

Protextor, A. (2008) 'Readers Comments', *Film Comment*, http://tinyurl.
com/3a4s5mw (accessed 24 June 2008).

Reesman, B. (2008) 'Dario Argento: The Horror Within', *MovieMaker*,
15, 76, 71–2.

Sayre, N. (1974) 'Bring Me the Head of Alfredo Garcia', *New York Times*,
http://tinyurl.com/367xpbk (accessed 10 October 2007).

Schager, N. (2005) '*Bring Me the Head of Alfredo Garcia*', *Slant Magazine*, http://tinyurl.com/3y8zevt (accessed 24 June 2008).

Sconce, J. (2003) '"Trashing" the academy: Taste, excess and an
emerging politics of cinematic style', in E. Mathijs and X. Mendik
(eds) *The Cult Film Reader*. New York: McGraw Hill Open University
Press, 100–18.

Seydor, P. (1980) *Peckinpah: The Western Films*. Urbana, Chicago and
London: University of Illinois Press.

Sherman, L. (2009) 'Guilty Pleasure: *Beyond the Valley of the Dolls*', *Spec-
trum Culture*, http://tinyurl.com/93x5h6 (accessed 14 February 2009).

Simmons, G. (1998) *Peckinpah: A Portrait in Montage*. New York: Lime-
light Editions.

Smith, G. (1993) 'The Gambler, an Interview with Abel Ferrara', *Sight &
Sound*, 3, 2, 20–3.

Speruzzi, W. (2007) 'Intoxicated with the Madness', *This Savage Art*, http://tinyurl.com/3ypll4t/ (accessed 2 April 2008).

Spoto, D. (1983) *The Dark Side of Genius. The Life of Alfred Hitchcock*. London: Frederick Muller.

Sragow, M. (2000a) 'Lear meets the energy vampire', *Salon.com*, http://tinyurl.com/3xjvdjj (accessed 10 October 2008).

____ (2000b) '*Deliverance*', *Salon.com*, http://tinyurl.com/38xe5rf (accessed 10 October 2008).

Taylor, D. J. (2003) 'Gordon Who?', *Guardian*, http://tinyurl.com/2wotmo3 (accessed 13 June 2009).

Telotte, J. P. (2003) '*The Blair Witch Project*: Film and the Internet', in E. Mathijs and X. Mendik (eds) *The Cult Film Reader*. New York: McGraw Hill Open University Press, 263–73.

thevoid99 (2007) '*The Man Who Fell to Earth*', *epinions.com*, http://tinyurl.com/36sh5cy (accessed 10 October 2007).

Thomson, D. (2002a) 'Film Studies: Paranoid and violent – Peckinpah comes back to haunt us', *Independent*, http://tinyurl.com/2wfsor8 (accessed 10 October 2008).

____ (2002b) *The New Biographical Dictionary of Film: 4th Edition*. London: Little, Brown.

____ (2004a) 'Film Studies: Dark, depressive, volatile – the film buff who lost the plot', *Independent*, 11 July, 13.

____ (2004b) *The Whole Equation*. London: Little, Brown.

____ (2009) 'Sam Peckinpah: Dead Men Walking', *Sight & Sound*, 19, 2, 32–6.

von Busack, R. (1998) 'A Bag of Loot', *Metroactive Movies*, http://tinyurl.com/2v9bs4j (accessed 19 February 2009).

Walker, J. (ed.) (2001) *Halliwell's Film and Video Guide*. London: Collins.

Walsh, P. (2007) 'Rod Lurie plans "improvements" for Remake of Peckinpah's *Straw Dogs*', *Cinematical*, http://tinyurl.com/34u2qgn (accessed 10 October 2008).

Weddle, D. (1994) *"If They Move...Kill 'Em!" The Life and Times of Sam Peckinpah*. New York: Grove Press.

____ (1995) '*Straw Dogs*: They Want To See Brains Flying Out?', *Sight & Sound*, 5, 2, 20–5.

Wood, R. (1986) 'From Buddies to Lovers', in *Hollywood from Vietnam to Reagan*. New York: Columbia University Press, 222–44.

____ (1991) *Hitchcock's Films Revisited*. London: Faber and Faber.

INDEX